SuccessMaker

SuccessMaker Targeted Lessons
Fractions and Decimals

Student Practice

Glenview, Illinois; Boston, Massachusetts; Chandler, Arizona; New York, New York
SuccessMaker.com
800-848-9500

Copyright © 2018 Pearson Education, Inc., or its affiliates. All Rights Reserved. Printed in the United States of America. This publication is protected by copyright and permission should be obtained from the publisher prior to any prohibited reproduction, storage in a retrieval system, or transmission in any form or by any means, electronic, mechanical, photocopying, recording, or likewise. The publisher hereby grants permission to reproduce student pages, in part or in whole, for classroom use only, the number not to exceed the number of students in each class. Notice of copyright will appear on all copies. For information regarding permissions, request forms, and the appropriate contacts within the Pearson Education Global Rights & Permission department, please visit www.pearsoned.com/permissions/.

ISBN-13: 978-0-328-99160-0
ISBN-10: 0-328-99160-0

Contents

1	Identifying Fractions Using Sets	1
2	Identifying Fractions Using Area Models	7
3	Unit Fractions	11
4	Fractions Using Number Lines	13
5	Fractions Using Models	17
6	Equivalent Fraction Area Models	21
7	Equivalent Fraction Set Models	27
8	Equivalent Fraction Linear Models	31
9	Whole Number Fractions	37
10	Comparing Fractions	39
11	More Comparing Fractions	47
12	Ordering Fractions	49
13	Fractions and Mixed Numbers	53
14	Simplifying Fractions	59
15	Adding Fractions with Like Denominators	71
16	Subtracting Fractions with Like Denominators	77
17	Adding and Subtracting Fractions with Unlike Denominators	83
18	Adding Mixed Numbers with Like Denominators	93
19	Subtracting Mixed Numbers with Like Denominators	101
20	Adding and Subtracting Mixed Numbers with Unlike Denominators	109

FRACTIONS AND DECIMALS

Contents

21	Multiplying Fractions by Whole Numbers	115
22	Multiplying Fractions	121
23	Dividing Unit Fractions	133
24	Dividing by Unit Fractions	137
25	Fraction Operations Word Problems	141
26	Representing Tenths and Hundredths	145
27	Decimals and the Zero	149
28	Powers of Ten	153
29	Equivalent Decimals and Fractions	159
30	Comparing Decimals	165
31	Ordering Decimals	175
32	Estimating Decimal Operations	179
33	Decimal Sequences	185
34	Adding and Subtracting Decimals	193
35	Multiplying Decimals	205
36	Multiplying and Dividing Decimals	217
37	Decimal Operations Word Problems	227

Identifying Fractions Using Sets

show me

12 ÷ 3 = _____

setting the direction

> **example**
>
> Share 12 eggs equally between 2 people.
> Sketch a diagram to show your result.
>
>
>
> person 1   person 2

work time

1. a. Share 12 eggs equally among 3 people.
   Use counters to show this.
   Then make a drawing to show your result.

   b. How many of the 12 eggs does each person get?

   ◎ Write your answer as a complete sentence.

FRACTIONS AND DECIMALS

1 Identifying Fractions Using Sets

c. Share 12 eggs equally among 4 people. Use counters to show this. Then make a drawing to show your result.

d. How many of the 12 eggs does each person get?

2. Get page 5 and cut out the pictures of ribbons.

> **example**
>
> Share 1 ribbon equally between 2 people.
> How much of the whole ribbon does each person get?
>
> Each person gets $\frac{1}{2}$ of the whole ribbon.
>
> Write the amount $\frac{1}{2}$ on each piece. Paste the 2 pieces below.

a. Cut 1 ribbon to share equally between 4 people. Paste your 4 pieces below.

b. How much of the whole ribbon does each person get?

c. Write the amount as a fraction on each piece.

3. a. Share another ribbon equally among 8 people. Paste your 8 pieces below.

   b. How much of the whole ribbon does each person get?

   c. Write the amount as a fraction on each piece.

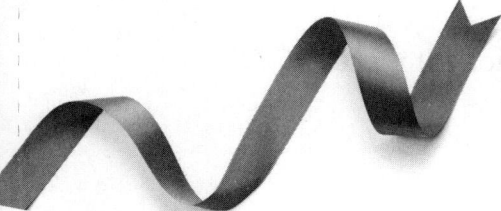

4. a. Share another ribbon equally among 3 people. Paste your 3 pieces below.

   b. How much of the whole ribbon does each person get?

   c. Write the amount as a fraction on each piece.

1 Identifying Fractions Using Sets

5. Look at your answers to the ribbon-sharing problems and the example.

   a. How many people were sharing when they each got the longest pieces of ribbon?

   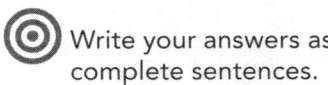 Write your answers as complete sentences.

   b. How many people were sharing when they each got the shortest pieces of ribbon?

↩ reflection

Two everyday situations in which I see fractions are …

_____
_____
_____
_____
_____
_____
_____

SHARING RIBBONS

Identifying Fractions Using Area Models

show me

4 ÷ 2 = _____

setting the direction

example

In art class, 2 friends shared this piece of clay equally.

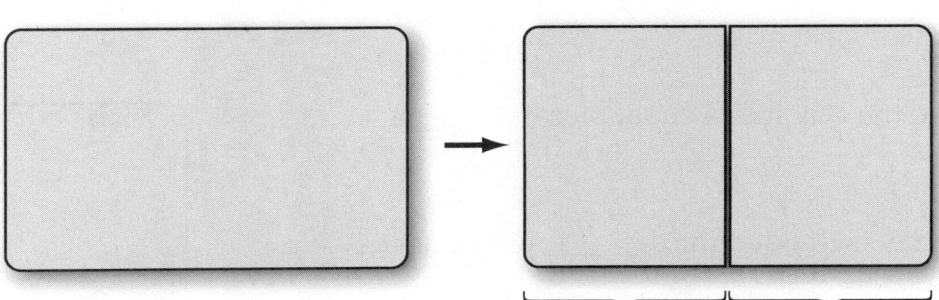

This is 1 whole piece of clay.

one-half $\frac{1}{2}$ one-half $\frac{1}{2}$

These pieces are $\frac{1}{2}$ of a whole piece.

There are 2 pieces of size $\frac{1}{2}$.

This piece of clay is divided into 2 pieces, but the pieces are not equal.

Neither one is $\frac{1}{2}$ of the whole piece.

2 Identifying Fractions Using Area Models

⟳ work time

1. a. Divide the clay into 3 equal pieces.

   b. This clay is divided into _____ pieces of size $\frac{1}{3}$.

   c. If 3 people share the clay equally, each person gets _____ of the whole piece.

2. a. Divide the clay into 4 equal pieces.

   b. This clay is divided into _____ pieces of size $\frac{1}{4}$.

   c. If 4 people share the clay equally, each person gets _____ of the whole piece.

3. a. Divide the clay into 6 equal pieces.

   b. This clay is divided into _____ pieces of size $\frac{1}{6}$.

   c. If 6 people share the clay equally, each person gets _____ of the whole piece.

FRACTIONS AND DECIMALS

4. Divide the clay into 2 equal pieces, but cut it a different way than as in the example.

reflection

I use fractions to …

Unit Fractions 3

show me

This arrow shows _____ of the distance from 0 to 1.

work time

1. Fill in the blanks in this table.

Diagram	Number of Equal Parts	What Is Shaded	I Say	I Write
	___ equal parts	1 out of _2_ equal parts		
	___ equal parts	1 out of ___ equal parts		
	___ equal parts	1 out of ___ equal parts		$\frac{1}{4}$
	_6_ equal parts	1 out of ___ equal parts		
	___ equal parts	1 out of ___ equal parts	one-eighth	

FRACTIONS AND DECIMALS

3 Unit Fractions

reflection

As the number of equal parts increases, each part…

Fractions Using Number Lines

show me

What part of this circle is shaded?

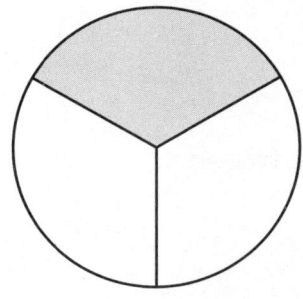

setting the direction

How many hops of $\frac{1}{4}$ does this arrow show?

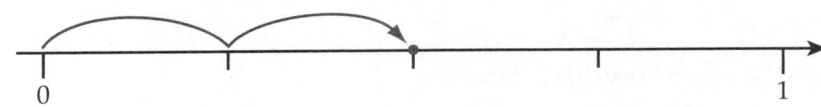

Label each hop with a fraction.

> **example**
>
> The arrow on the number line shows 2 hops of $\frac{1}{4}$.
>
> As a fraction, this is written $\frac{2}{4}$.
>
> In this fraction, 2 is the numerator (the number of equal parts), and 4 is the denominator (the number of parts to make the whole).

4 Fractions Using Number Lines

work time

1. a. How many hops of $\frac{1}{4}$ does this arrow show?

   b. Label each hop with a fraction.

2. a. How many hops of $\frac{1}{6}$ does this arrow show?

   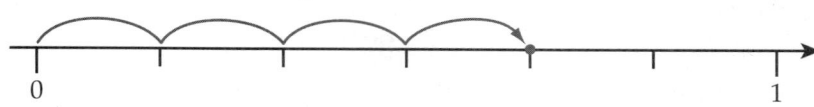

   b. Label each hop with a fraction.

3. a. How many hops of $\frac{1}{8}$ does this arrow show?

   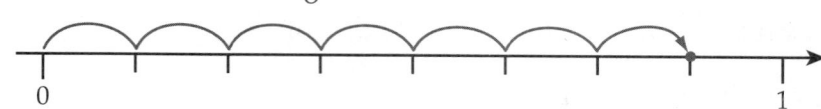

   b. Label each hop with a fraction.

4.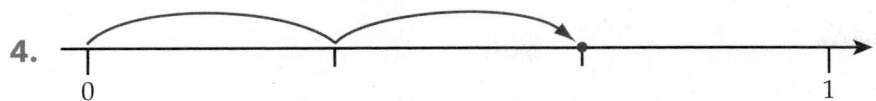

Label each hop with a fraction.

5.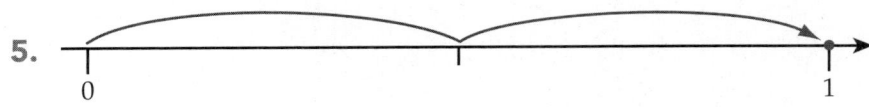

Label each hop with a fraction.

6. Mark $\frac{5}{6}$ on this number line.

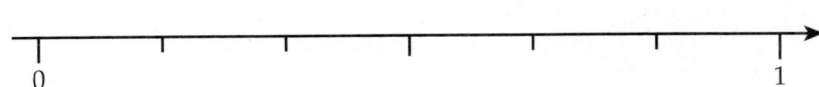

reflection

Using a number line to show fractions helps me …

_____
_____
_____
_____

Fractions Using Area Models

show me

Write the fraction that is shown by this arrow.

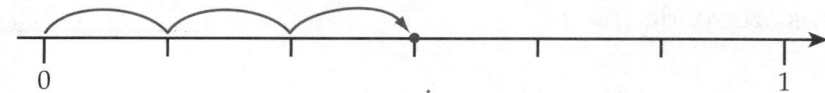

work time

1. a. How many equal pieces is this circle divided into?

    b. What is the size of each piece?

    c. How many pieces are shaded?

    d. Write the fraction that tells what part of the circle is shaded.

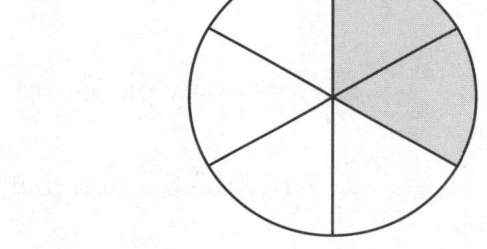

5 Fractions Using Area Models

2. a. How many equal pieces is this square divided into?

    b. What is the size of each piece?

    c. How many pieces are shaded?

    d. Write the fraction that tells what part of the square is shaded.

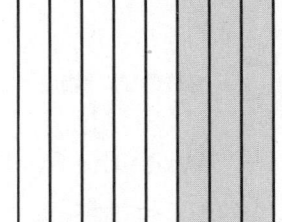

3. a. How many equal pieces is this rectangle divided into?

    b. What is the size of each piece?

    c. How many pieces are shaded?

    d. Write the fraction that tells what part of the rectangle is shaded.

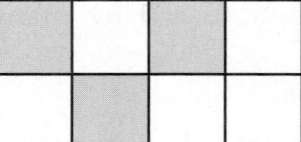

4. a. How many equal pieces is this triangle divided into?

    b. What is the size of each piece?

    c. How many pieces are shaded?

    d. Write the fraction that tells what part of the triangle is shaded.

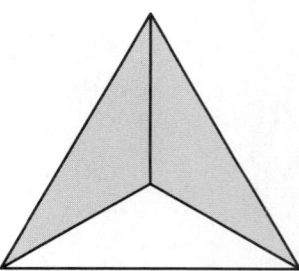

5. a. Compare your answers to problems 2 and 3. What is the same?

b. What is different?

⊃ reflection

I can draw an area model of $\frac{5}{8}$ like this...

Equivalent Fraction Area Models

show me

Show me $\frac{3}{8}$ in a diagram.

setting the direction

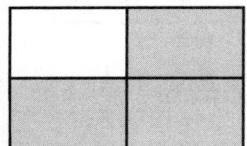 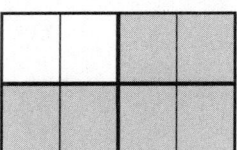

Equation: $\frac{3}{4} = \frac{6}{8}$

Draw lines to divide the area into equal parts in another way. Write an equation that shows the result.

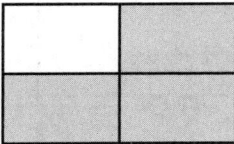

Equation: $\frac{3}{4} =$

6 Equivalent Fraction Area Models

⟳ work time

1. Draw lines to divide the area into equal parts in at least three ways. Write an equation that shows the result.

a.

Equation: $\dfrac{1}{2} =$

b.

Equation: $\dfrac{1}{2} =$

c.

Equation:

d.

Equation:

Equivalent Fraction Area Models

2. Draw lines to divide the area into equal parts in two ways. Write an equation that shows the result.

   a.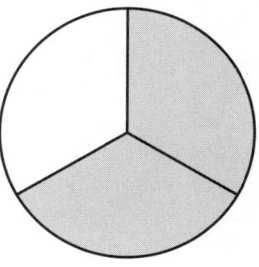

   Equation: $\dfrac{2}{3} =$

   b.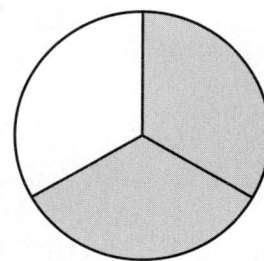

   Equation:

3. Draw lines to divide the area into equal parts in another way. Write an equation that shows the result.

   Equation:

Equivalent Fraction Area Models

4. Tran drew a rectangular area model to show a fraction and then covered most of it with a piece of paper.

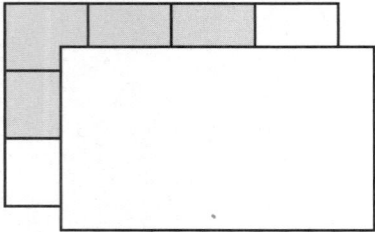

Write some fractions that Tran's model might represent.

Shade the blank diagrams to show why your fractions make sense.

   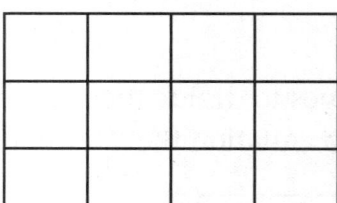

   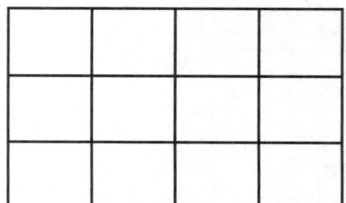

Equivalent Fraction Area Models

↻ reflection

Today I learned …

Equivalent Fraction Set Models

show me

Sketch a diagram that shows $\frac{1}{5}$ of a set shaded.

setting the direction

example

Malaya made a fruit salad with 6 strawberries and 6 green grapes.

What fraction of Malaya's fruit salad is strawberries? What fraction is grapes?

- Group the fruits in as many ways as you can to make different fraction names.
- Use diagrams to show your thinking.

Diagram		Diagram	
(6 strawberries circled, 6 grapes circled)	$\frac{1}{2}$ Strawberries $\frac{1}{2}$ Grapes		Strawberries Grapes

Diagram		Diagram	
	Strawberries Grapes		Strawberries Grapes

Fraction names for strawberries: $\dfrac{1}{2} = \dfrac{}{} = \dfrac{}{} = \dfrac{}{}$

Fraction names for grapes: $\dfrac{1}{2} = \dfrac{}{} = \dfrac{}{} = \dfrac{}{}$

FRACTIONS AND DECIMALS

7 Equivalent Fraction Set Models

work time

1. Josh made a fruit salad using 12 fruits, too. Josh's fruit salad used 8 strawberries and 4 green grapes.

   What fraction of Josh's fruit salad is strawberries? What fraction is grapes?

   - Group the fruits in as many ways as you can to make different fraction names.
   - Use diagrams to show your thinking.

Diagram	Strawberries Grapes	Diagram	Strawberries Grapes
Diagram	Strawberries Grapes	Diagram	Strawberries Grapes

Fraction names for strawberries: ―― = ―― = ――

Fraction names for grapes: ―― = ―― = ――

Equivalent Fraction Set Models 7

2. Anna made a bigger fruit salad using 24 fruits. Anna used 8 green grapes and 16 strawberries.

What fraction of Anna's fruit salad is strawberries? What fraction is grapes?

- Group the fruits in as many ways as you can to make different fraction names.
- Use diagrams to show your thinking.

Diagram	Strawberries Grapes	Diagram	Strawberries Grapes
Diagram	Strawberries Grapes	Diagram	Strawberries Grapes

Fraction names for strawberries: ____ = ____ = ____ = ____

Fraction names for grapes: ____ = ____ = ____ = ____

FRACTIONS AND DECIMALS   29

7 Equivalent Fraction Set Models

3. Circle the names of the two people whose fruit salads are the most alike:

Malaya   Josh   Anna

Why did you chose those two people?

reflection

I like using set models for fractions because . . .

Equivalent Fraction Linear Models

show me

Sketch a line segment that shows $\frac{9}{4}$ inches.

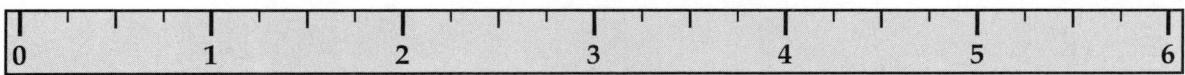

work time

1. Use your ruler to help you find a fraction equivalent to each fraction below.

   a. $\frac{6}{8}$ b. $\frac{3}{2}$

2. Get page 35, *Paper Strips,* and cut out both paper strips along the dashed lines.

   - Your teacher will tell you how to fold the strips.
   - As you fold your strips, use them to help you complete the number lines on page 32.
   - Use your number lines to complete parts a–b that follow.

8 Equivalent Fraction Linear Models

a. Circle all of the sets of equivalent fractions on the number lines.

Equivalent Fraction Linear Models 8

b. Use equals signs (=) to show sets of equivalent fractions using symbols.

8 Equivalent Fraction Linear Models

3. a. Think about what you have learned so far about equivalent fractions. Complete the following conjecture based on the patterns you observe in equivalent fractions:

- Conjecture: The numerators and denominators in equivalent fractions are related by what mathematical operation(s)? (List one or more.)

b. Write why you think your conjecture is true. Include an example in your explanation.

reflection

I understand equivalent fractions because . . .

_____

_____

_____

_____

PAPER STRIPS

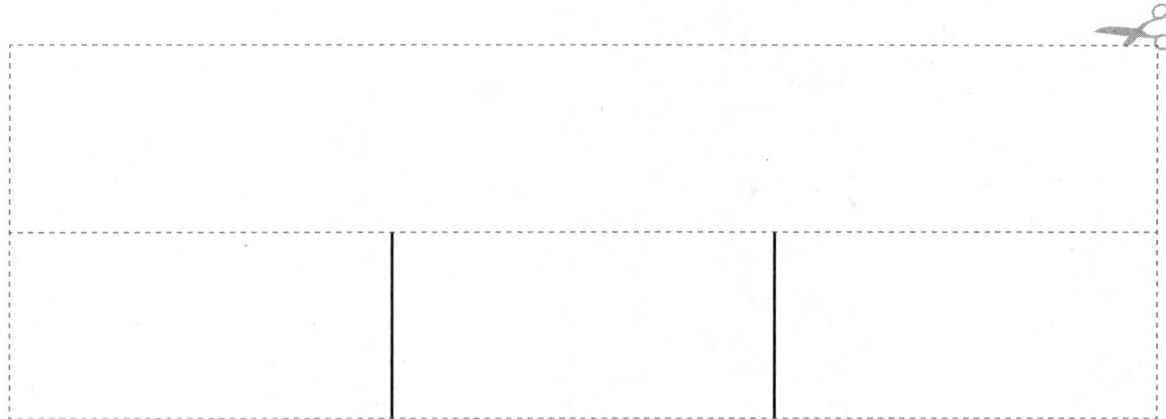

Do not cut the solid lines.

Whole Number Fractions

show me

Write a fraction equivalent to $\frac{3}{6}$.

setting the direction

example

How many fourths does this number line show?

$\frac{1}{4}$ $\frac{2}{4}$ $\frac{3}{4}$ $\frac{4}{4}$ $\frac{5}{4}$ $\frac{6}{4}$ $\frac{7}{4}$ $\frac{8}{4}$

0 — 1 — 2

work time

1. a. At their work table, 4 students open a box of 4 pencils and share them equally. How many pencils does each student get?

   b. Write three different fractions that are all equal to 1.

2. The fraction $\frac{2}{2}$ is 2 one-halves, and the fraction $\frac{2}{4}$ is 2 one-fourths.

   a. What whole number is $\frac{2}{1}$?

   b. What whole number is $\frac{4}{2}$?

◎ Use a ruler or number line if you need help.

Whole Number Fractions

c. What whole number is $\frac{6}{2}$?

3. a. Mark and label these fractions on the number line below.

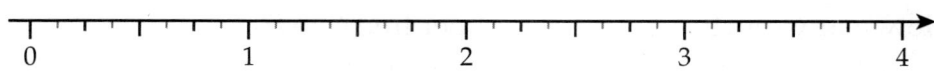

$$\frac{8}{4} \quad \frac{2}{1} \quad \frac{3}{1} \quad \frac{4}{4} \quad \frac{4}{1} \quad \frac{6}{8} \quad \frac{2}{2}$$

4. Which one of the fractions above is different from all the others? Explain your answer.

reflection

One thing that still confuses me is …

_____

_____

_____

Comparing Fractions

⤳ show me

Write a fraction equivalent to $\frac{2}{3}$.

⤳ work time

1. Get page 41 and cut out all of the cards.

    - On each card, shade the diagram to match the fraction, or write a fraction to match the shaded area.

    - When all the cards are completed, sort them in order from least to greatest.

    - Compare your ordering with your partner's. Explain to your partner how you know that the card order is correct. Your partner should either agree with your explanation or challenge it if your explanation is not clear, correct, and complete.

    - When you are sure you have the cards in the correct order, attach them in order below.

Comparing Fractions

2. Get page 43 and cut out all of the cards.

   - On each card, mark the number line to match the given fraction, or write a fraction to match the number line.

   - When all the cards are completed, sort them in order from least to greatest.

   - Compare your ordering with your partner's. Explain to your partner how you know that the card order is correct. Your partner should either agree with your explanation or challenge it if your explanation is not clear, correct, and complete.

   - When you are sure the cards are in the correct order, attach them in order below.

AREA CARDS

$\frac{4}{8}$ $\frac{7}{8}$ $\frac{1}{8}$

FRACTIONS AND DECIMALS 41

NUMBER LINE CARDS

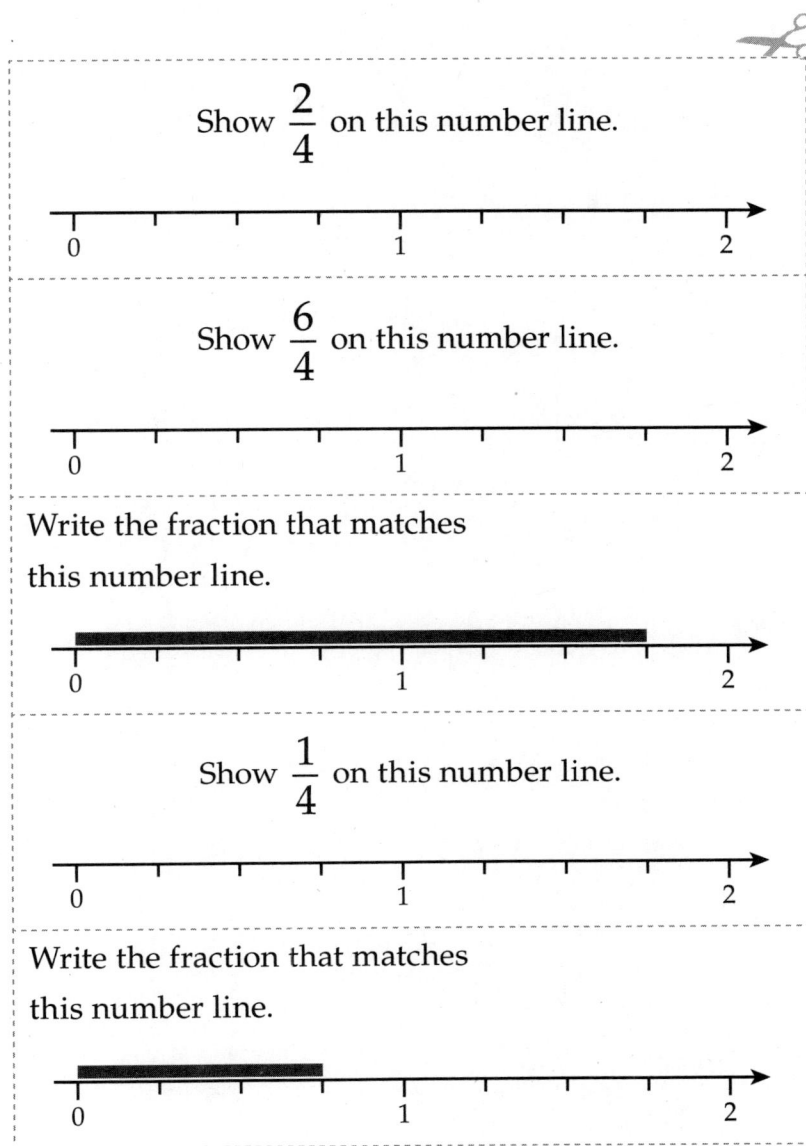

3. a. Which is greater, $\frac{1}{2}$ or $\frac{1}{4}$?

   b. Which is more pizza, $\frac{1}{2}$ of the small pizza or $\frac{1}{4}$ of the large pizza?

   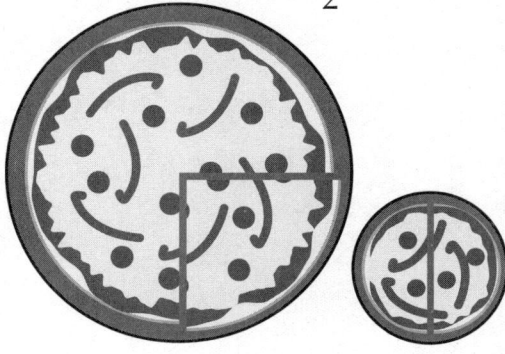

   c. What does that tell you about comparing fractions?

reflection

When I see two fractions with the same denominator, I know which is greater by …

More Comparing Fractions

show me

Which is greater, $\frac{2}{8}$ or $\frac{3}{8}$?

work time

1. a. Write the following fractions in order from least to greatest.

    $\frac{1}{2}$ $\frac{1}{8}$ $\frac{1}{3}$ $\frac{1}{6}$ $\frac{1}{4}$

    Least   Greatest

    b. Draw area models below to match the five fractions above.
       Show them in the same order, from least to greatest.

11 More Comparing Fractions

2. a. Mark points on the number line below to match the following fractions.

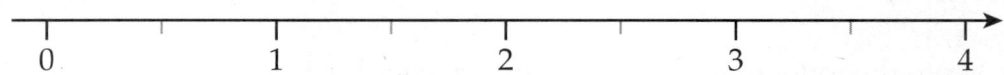

b. Write the fractions above the points you marked.

3. If you see two different fractions with the same numerator, how do you know which fraction is greater?

reflection

I would rather earn $\frac{3}{4}$ of a dollar than $\frac{3}{8}$ of a dollar because…

Ordering Fractions

12

show me

Which is greater, $\frac{4}{6}$ or $\frac{5}{6}$?

work time

1. Get page 51 and cut out all of the cards.

   a. Work with your partner:
      i. Draw a large number line from 0 to 2 on your poster paper. Label 0, 1, and 2 on your number line.
      ii. Sort the fraction cards in order from least to greatest. Make sure you both agree.
      iii. Attach the fractions to your poster.
      iv. If you have time, write some more fractions that go between others already on your number line and place them in the correct order.

reflection

One strategy that I found useful in putting fractions in order is …

_____
_____
_____
_____
_____

FRACTIONS TO PUT IN ORDER

$\frac{3}{6}$	$\frac{6}{3}$	$\frac{1}{8}$	$\frac{6}{4}$	$\frac{2}{1}$	$\frac{3}{4}$
$\frac{2}{3}$	$\frac{1}{3}$	$\frac{4}{4}$	$\frac{5}{6}$	$\frac{4}{8}$	$\frac{1}{4}$
$\frac{2}{6}$	$\frac{1}{2}$	$\frac{8}{4}$	$\frac{2}{8}$	$\frac{4}{6}$	$\frac{6}{8}$
$\frac{2}{4}$	$\frac{4}{2}$	$\frac{1}{6}$	$\frac{3}{3}$		

Fractions and Mixed Numbers

show me

Write an equation for what the number line shows.

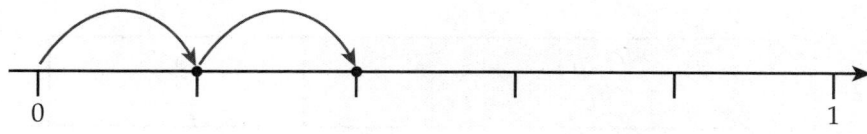

setting the direction

example

$\frac{5}{6}$ is called a *proper fraction* because its numerator is less than its denominator. A proper fraction is always a number less than 1.

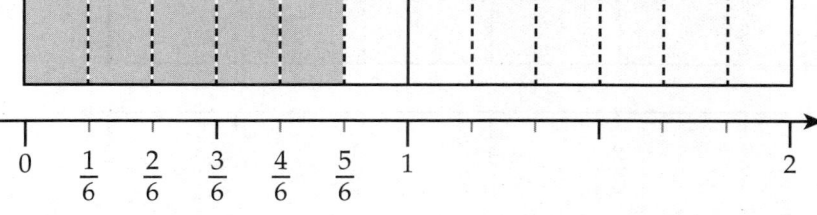

FRACTIONS AND DECIMALS

13 Fractions and Mixed Numbers

example

$\frac{4}{3}$ is called an *improper fraction* because its numerator is greater than its denominator. An improper fraction has a numerator that is greater than or equal to its denominator, so an improper fraction is always greater than or equal to 1.

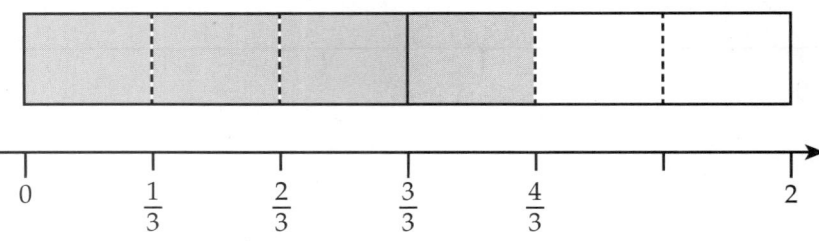

example

$1\frac{2}{3}$ is called a *mixed number fraction* because it is the sum of a whole number and a fraction: $1 + \frac{2}{3} = 1\frac{2}{3}$.

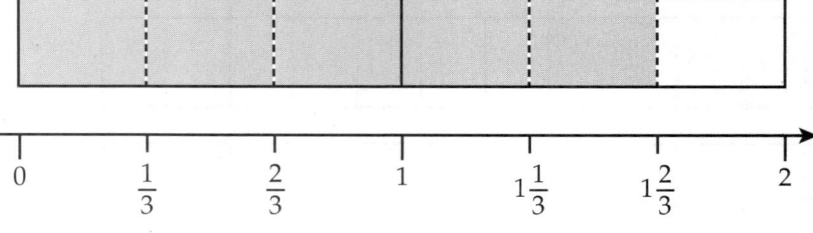

⇨ work time

1. Work with a partner.

   - Get page 57, *Fractions and Mixed Numbers*, and cut out all the cards.

   - Take turns sorting the cards so that you have four representations of the same fraction or mixed number.

   - Explain to your partner how you know that the cards match. Your partner should either agree with your explanation or challenge it if your explanation is not clear, correct, and complete.

   - Once you have grouped the cards, arrange each group in a row, starting with the numeral, then the tape diagram, then the number line, and then the expression.

   example

   $\frac{4}{5}$ |tape diagram| |number line| $\frac{1}{5} + \frac{1}{5} + \frac{1}{5} + \frac{1}{5} = \frac{4}{5}$

   - Once you and your partner believe your cards are sorted and arranged correctly, ask your teacher to check them. Your teacher will then tell you if you can tape each row of cards together.

   - Arrange the rows of cards so they show the fractions and mixed numbers from least to greatest.

13 Fractions and Mixed Numbers

2. Write an improper fraction and a mixed number for what the tape diagram shows.

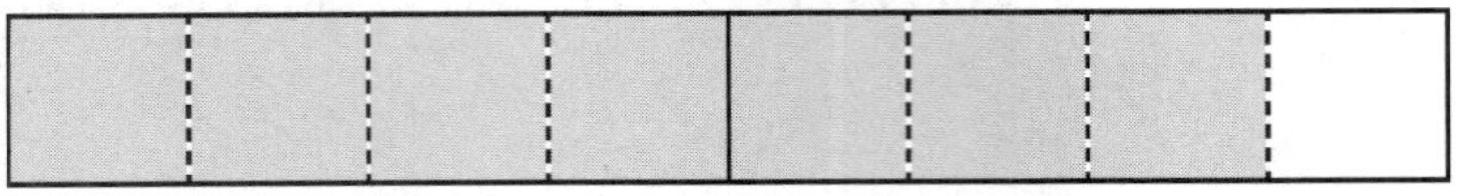

Improper fraction: _____

Mixed number: _____

↻ reflection

The difference between a proper fraction, an improper fraction, and a mixed number is…

_____
_____
_____
_____
_____
_____
_____
_____

FRACTIONS AND MIXED NUMBERS

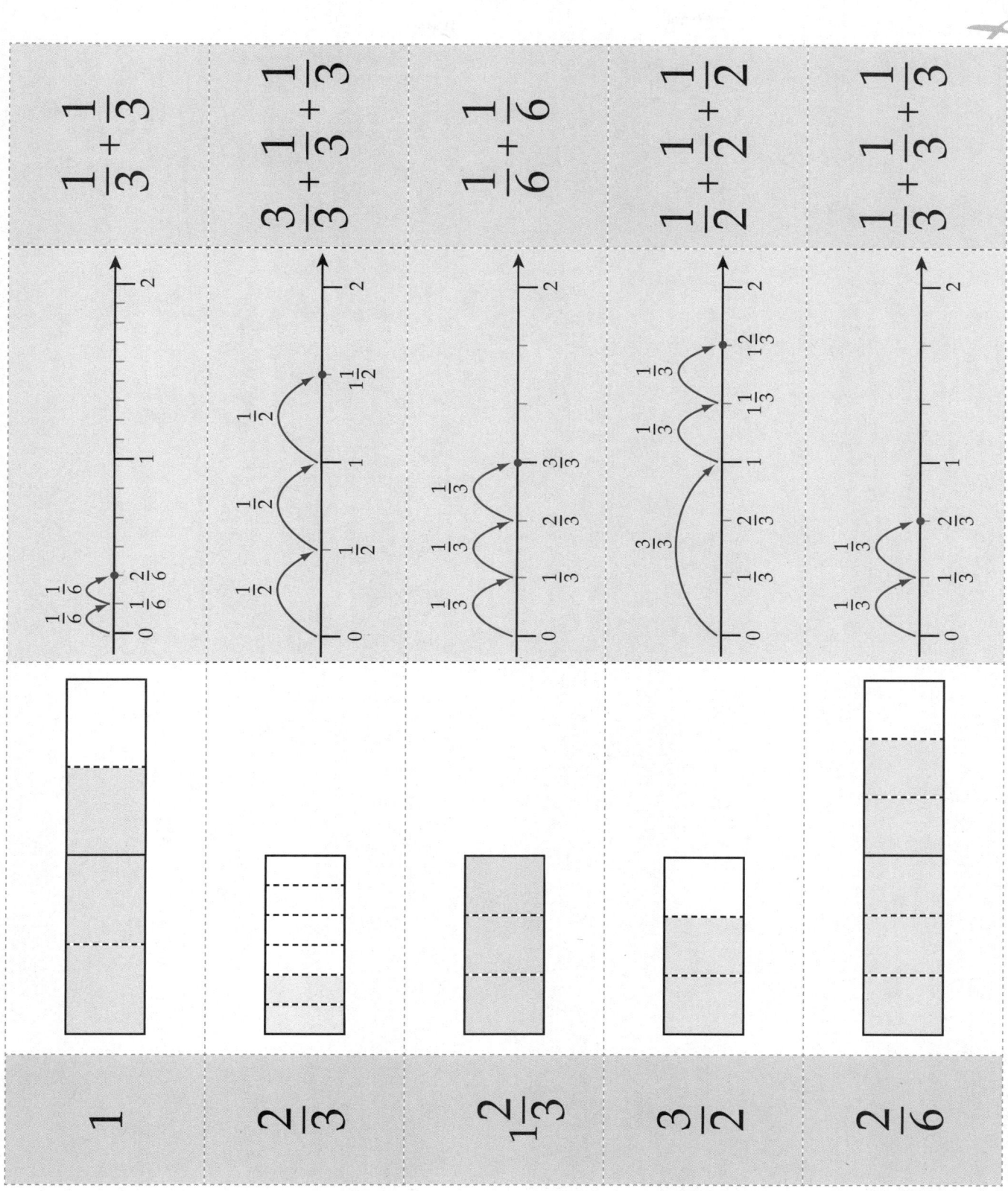

Simplifying Fractions

⤴ show me

Show me at least two fractions or mixed numbers that are equivalent to $\frac{30}{24}$.

⤴ setting the direction

Place the fractions below in the proper columns in the chart.

$$\frac{4}{7} \quad 3\frac{1}{3} \quad 6\frac{2}{8} \quad \frac{62}{8} \quad \frac{502}{505} \quad \frac{1,001}{1,000}$$

Proper Fractions	Improper Fractions	Mixed Numbers

FRACTIONS AND DECIMALS

14 Simplifying Fractions

work time

1. Work with a partner. You will need scissors and tape.

   - Get pages 61, 63, and 65, *Hexagon Fractions*, and cut out all of the triangles.

   - Take turns matching a fraction or mixed number on one triangle with an equivalent fraction or mixed number on another triangle.

   - Explain to your partner how you know the calculation matches the answer. Your partner should either agree or challenge your explanation, if it is not clear, correct, and complete.

   - When you both agree, tape the matching edges of the triangles together.

   - Continue until all the pieces are together in one large hexagon with matching equivalent fractions or mixed numbers opposite each other.

   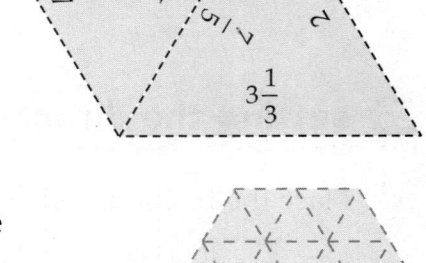

   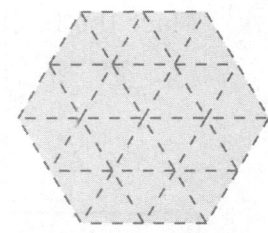

   If you need help, get page 67, *Number Lines*, and use it to show your calculations.

2. Explain one method that you use to change an improper fraction to a mixed number.

HEXAGON FRACTIONS—1 OF 3

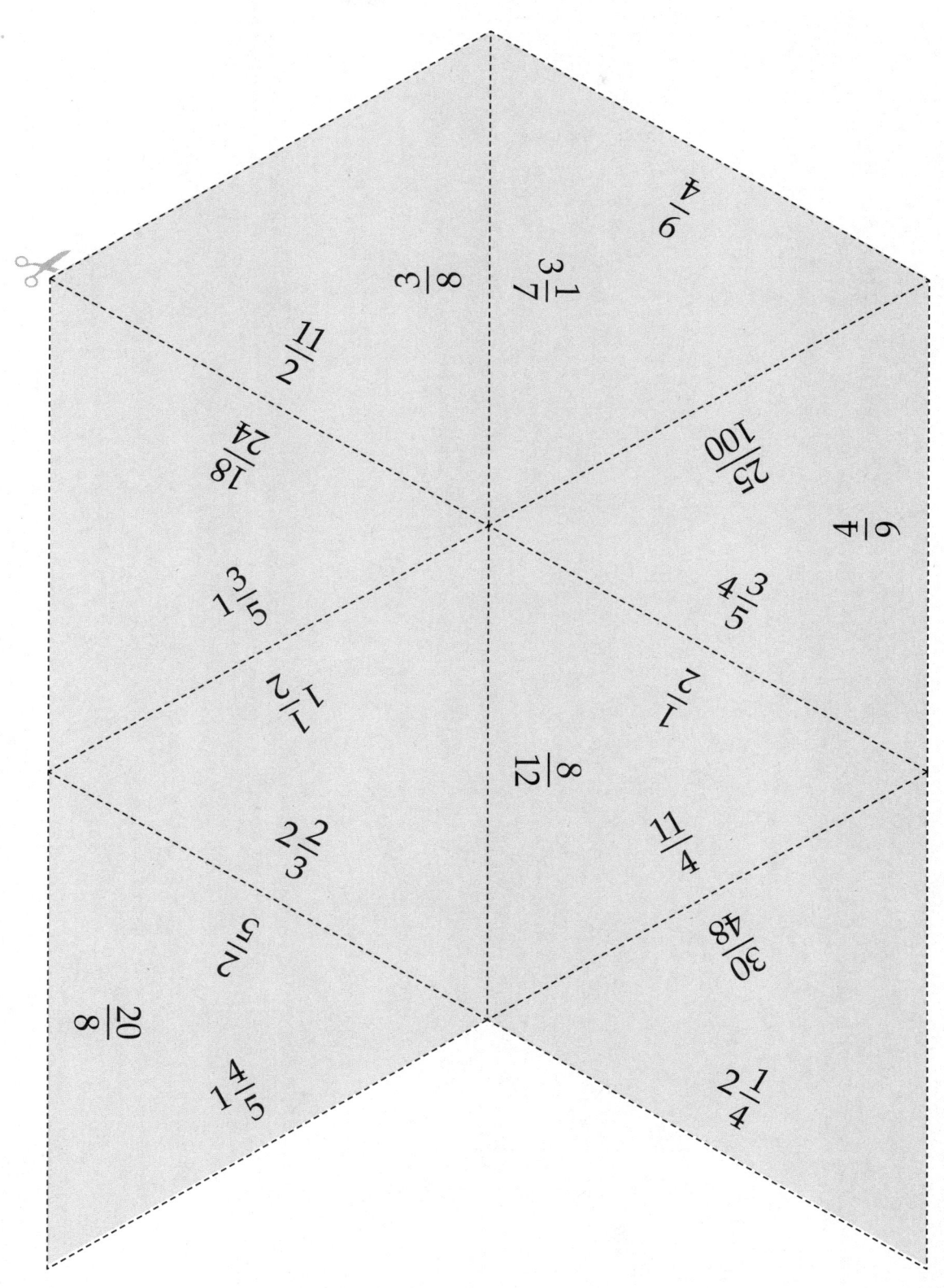

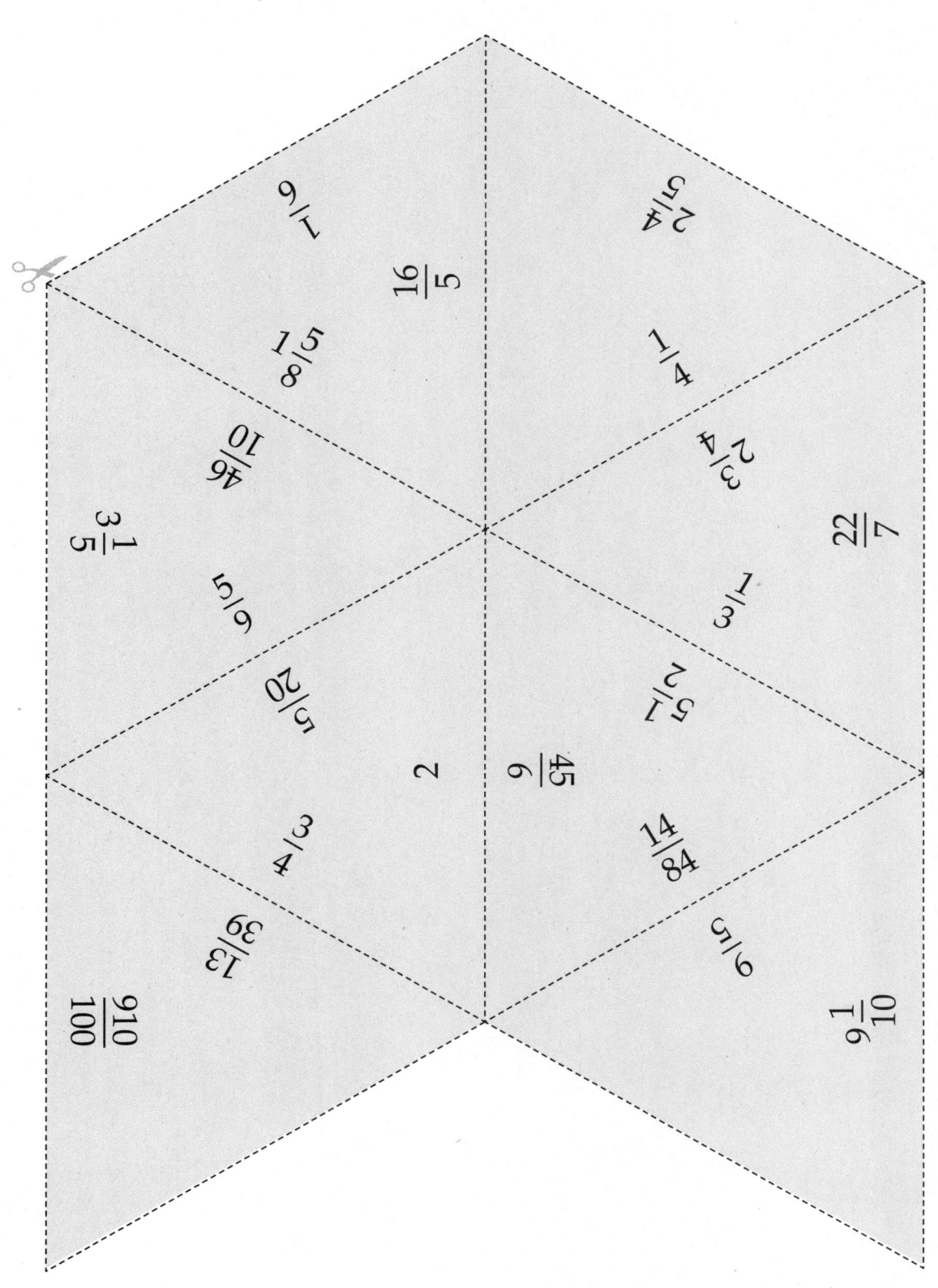

HEXAGON FRACTIONS—3 OF 3

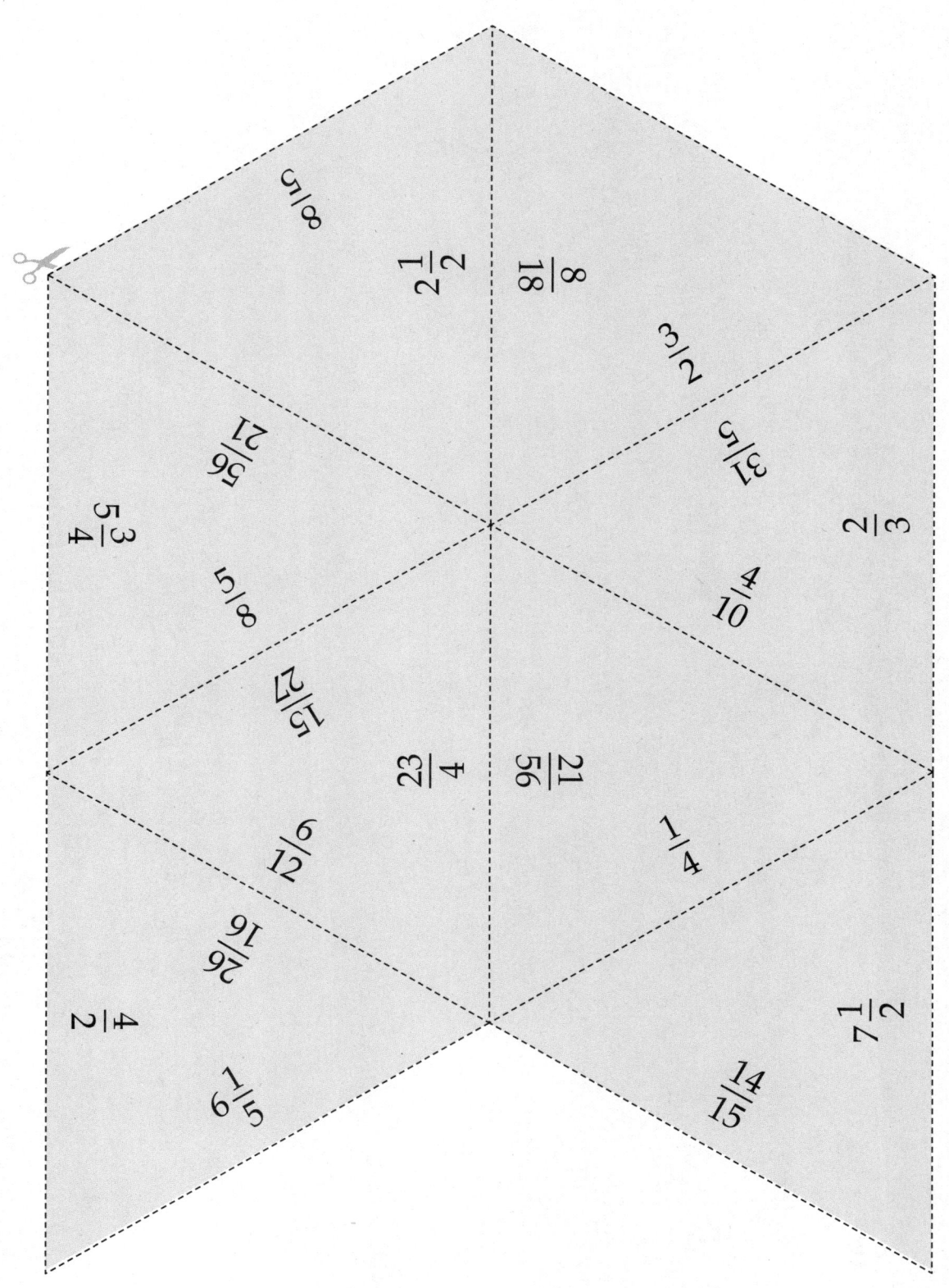

NUMBER LINES

FRACTIONS AND DECIMALS

3. How can you tell if a fraction is in simplest form?

⟶ reflection
....

The thing I found most helpful for putting together the hexagon puzzle was...

Adding Fractions with Like Denominators

15

⤷ show me

What mixed number does the point on the number line show?

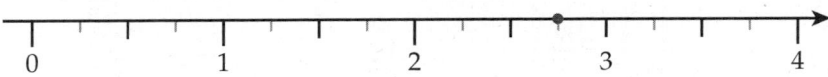

⤷ setting the direction

You know how to show addition on a number line.

How many lengths of $\frac{1}{4}$ make $1\frac{1}{4}$?

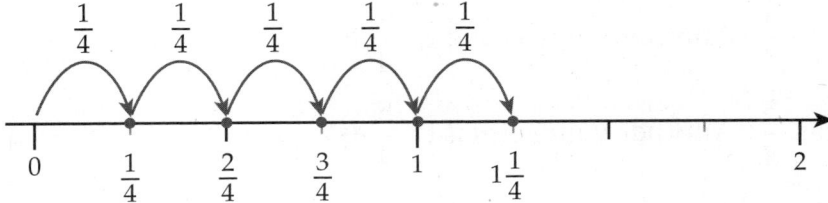

There are 5 lengths of $\frac{1}{4}$ that make $1\frac{1}{4}$.

$\frac{1}{4} + \frac{1}{4} + \frac{1}{4} + \frac{1}{4} + \frac{1}{4} = \frac{5}{4}$ or $1\frac{1}{4}$

15 Adding Fractions with Like Denominators

A tape diagram can also show how many parts of $\frac{1}{4}$ make $1\frac{1}{4}$. Look at this tape diagram and number line.

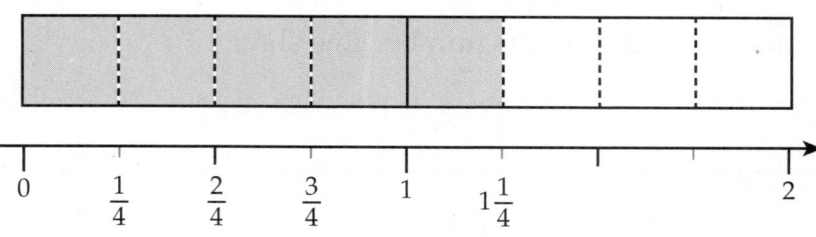

On the tape diagram, 1 whole is divided into ____ equal parts.

Each part is ____ of the whole.

You can write 4 parts of $\frac{1}{4}$ as $\frac{4}{4}$. Another value equal to $\frac{4}{4}$ is 1.

You can write 5 parts of $\frac{1}{4}$ as $\frac{5}{4}$. Another value equal to $\frac{5}{4}$ is $1\frac{1}{4}$.

The tape diagram shows all of these addition equations:

$\frac{1}{4} + \frac{1}{4} + \frac{1}{4} + \frac{1}{4} + \frac{1}{4} = \frac{5}{4}$

$\frac{1}{4} + \frac{1}{4} + \frac{1}{4} + \frac{1}{4} + \frac{1}{4} = 1\frac{1}{4}$

$\frac{4}{4} + \frac{1}{4} = \frac{5}{4}$

$\frac{4}{4} + \frac{1}{4} = 1\frac{1}{4}$

Adding Fractions with Like Denominators 15

work time

1. a. Use the tape diagram to add 6 parts of $\frac{1}{5}$.

   b. Fill in the blanks.

   You can write 5 parts of $\frac{1}{5}$ as the fraction ____.

   5 parts of $\frac{1}{5}$ are the same as ____ whole.

   You can write 6 parts of $\frac{1}{5}$ as the fraction ____.

   You can write 6 parts of $\frac{1}{5}$ as the mixed number ____.

   c. Write at least two equations that tell about the addition that the tape diagram shows.

15 Adding Fractions with Like Denominators

2. a. Add these fractions. Use the tape diagram to show the addition.

$$\frac{3}{4} + \frac{3}{4} + \frac{3}{4} + \frac{3}{4} + \frac{3}{4} = \underline{}$$

b. Write the sum as a fraction. Use the tape diagram to help you.

c. Write the sum as a mixed number. Use the tape diagram to help you.

3. Gabby uses colored thread that comes in lengths of $\frac{3}{5}$ yard to make friendship bracelets. She plans to use 4 lengths of thread to make a bracelet. How many yards of thread does she need to make the bracelet?

Sketch a tape diagram and write an equation.

4. a. Choose a fraction with a denominator from 2 through 6.

   b. Add 7 of the fractions. Sketch a tape diagram to show the addition.

   c. Write an equation that shows the sum as a fraction.

   d. Write an equation that shows the sum as a mixed number.

15 Adding Fractions with Like Denominators

↻ reflection

Using a model helps me add fractions with like denominators because . . .

Subtracting Fractions with Like Denominators

⇒ show me

Write an improper fraction for what the tape diagram shows.

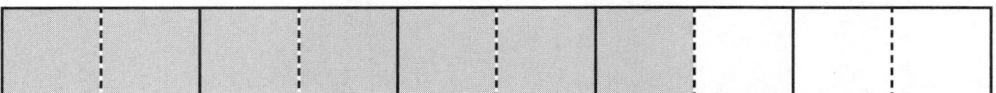

⇒ setting the direction

example

You can show subtraction of fractions on a number line.

$$\frac{7}{10} - \frac{3}{10} = \frac{4}{10}$$

7 lengths of $\frac{1}{10}$ minus 3 lengths of $\frac{1}{10}$ equals 4 lengths of $\frac{1}{10}$.

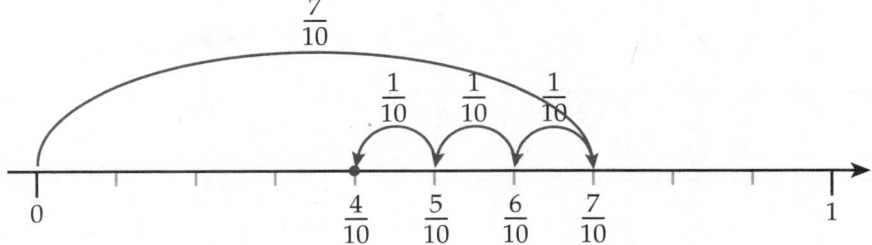

You can also show subtraction of fractions on a tape diagram. Look at this tape diagram and number line.

$$\frac{7}{10} - \frac{3}{10} = \frac{4}{10}$$

7 parts of $\frac{1}{10}$ minus 3 parts of $\frac{1}{10}$ equals 4 parts of $\frac{1}{10}$.

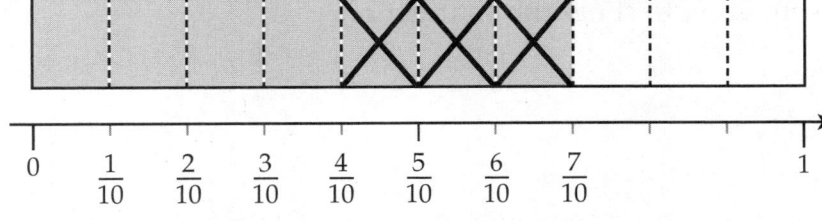

16 Subtracting Fractions with Like Denominators

work time

1. a. Use a tape diagram to find $\frac{4}{5} - \frac{3}{5}$.

   Shade to show 4 parts of $\frac{1}{5}$.

   b. Cross out to show subtracting 3 parts of $\frac{1}{5}$.

   c. Fill in the blanks to tell about the subtraction.

   _____ parts of $\frac{1}{5}$ minus _____ parts of $\frac{1}{5}$ equals _____ part of $\frac{1}{5}$.

   d. Complete the equation to show the subtraction.

   $\frac{4}{5} - \frac{3}{5} = \underline{}$

2. a. Use a number line to find $\frac{5}{8} - \frac{2}{8}$.

   Show subtracting 2 lengths of $\frac{1}{8}$.

   b. Fill in the blanks.

   _____ lengths of size $\frac{1}{8}$ minus _____ lengths of size $\frac{1}{8}$ equals _____ lengths of size $\frac{1}{8}$.

   c. Complete the equation to show the subtraction.

   $\frac{5}{8} - \frac{2}{8} = $ _____

3. Find $\frac{11}{12} - \frac{6}{12}$. Use a tape diagram or a number line to help you.
   Write your answer as an equation.

16 Subtracting Fractions with Like Denominators

4. Why can you use the following expressions to find $\frac{5}{6} - \frac{3}{6}$?

$$\frac{5}{6} - \frac{2}{6} - \frac{1}{6}$$

$$\frac{5}{6} - \frac{1}{6} - \frac{1}{6} - \frac{1}{6}$$

reflection

Using a model helps me subtract fractions because …

Adding and Subtracting Fractions with Unlike Denominators

setting the direction

Your teacher will write some fractions on the board. Which fractions on the board are equivalent to the fractions listed here?

$\dfrac{2}{6}$

$\dfrac{3}{6}$

$\dfrac{8}{12}$

$\dfrac{8}{20}$

Write two fractions that are equivalent to $\dfrac{1}{6}$.

Write two fractions that are equivalent to $\dfrac{3}{4}$.

17 Adding and Subtracting Fractions with Unlike Denominators

⤷ work time

1. Work with a partner. You will need scissors and tape.

   - Get page 85, *Shaded Areas*.

   - Take turns figuring out how much of each diagram is shaded and write your answers in the blanks.

   - Make sure to justify your calculations to your partner. Your partner should either agree with your explanation or challenge it if your explanation is not clear, correct, and complete.

   - When you have completed the sheet, get page 87, *Calculations*, and page 89, *Answers*.

   - Cut out the four cards on the *Shaded Areas* page, cut out all of the cards on the *Answers* page, and cut out the addition calculation cards on the *Calculations* page, but do not cut out the subtraction calculation cards yet.

   - Take turns matching the calculations with the answers and the shaded area diagrams.

     ◎ Each calculation matches one answer. Each shaded area diagram matches two pairs of addition calculations and answers and two pairs of subtraction calculations and answers.

   - Explain to your partner how you know the cards match. Your partner should either agree with your explanation or challenge it if the explanation is not clear, correct, and complete.

   - When you and your partner agree, tape the matching cards together.

   - When you finish the addition calculation cards, cut out all of the subtraction calculation cards and continue matching those cards with the answers and shaded area diagrams.

SHADED AREAS

1

_____ is shaded like this ☐.

_____ is shaded like this ☐.

So _____ is shaded altogether.

2

_____ is shaded like this ☐.

_____ is shaded like this ☐.

So _____ is shaded altogether.

3

_____ is shaded like this ☐.

_____ is shaded like this ☐.

So _____ is shaded altogether.

4

_____ is shaded like this ☐.

_____ is shaded like this ☐.

So _____ is shaded altogether.

CALCULATIONS

Addition Calculations

$\frac{1}{2} + \frac{1}{3} =$	$\frac{2}{5} + \frac{1}{4} =$	$\frac{2}{5} + \frac{1}{6} =$	$\frac{1}{4} + \frac{2}{3} =$
$\frac{1}{6} + \frac{2}{5} =$	$\frac{1}{3} + \frac{1}{2} =$	$\frac{1}{4} + \frac{2}{5} =$	$\frac{2}{3} + \frac{1}{4} =$

Subtraction Calculations

$\frac{11}{12} - \frac{2}{3} =$	$\frac{5}{6} - \frac{1}{3} =$	$\frac{17}{30} - \frac{1}{6} =$	$\frac{5}{6} - \frac{1}{2} =$
$\frac{17}{30} - \frac{2}{5} =$	$\frac{13}{20} - \frac{2}{5} =$	$\frac{11}{12} - \frac{1}{4} =$	$\frac{13}{20} - \frac{1}{4} =$

$\dfrac{5}{6}$	$\dfrac{2}{5}$	$\dfrac{1}{2}$	$\dfrac{13}{20}$
$\dfrac{1}{3}$	$\dfrac{11}{12}$	$\dfrac{1}{4}$	$\dfrac{17}{30}$
$\dfrac{13}{20}$	$\dfrac{1}{6}$	$\dfrac{5}{6}$	$\dfrac{2}{5}$
$\dfrac{11}{12}$	$\dfrac{2}{3}$	$\dfrac{1}{4}$	$\dfrac{17}{30}$

2. Explain the similarities and differences between $2\frac{8}{10}$; $2 + \frac{8}{10}$; 2.8; and $\frac{28}{10}$.

3. What have you learned about adding and subtracting fractions?

show me

- How many eighteenths is $\frac{2}{9}$? Show me your answer as an equation.

- How many eighteenths is $\frac{1}{6}$? Show me your answer as an equation.

- Solve for n. $\frac{2}{9} - \frac{1}{6} = n$

reflection

I understand adding and subtracting fractions best using: (circle one)

equations (such as $\frac{1}{3} + \frac{1}{6} = x$)   area models (such as ▭)

because…

18 Adding Mixed Numbers with Like Denominators

show me

Write an equation for which $\frac{4}{5}$ is the sum.

setting the direction

example

Tran uses a number line to add $3\frac{1}{4} + 2\frac{2}{4}$.

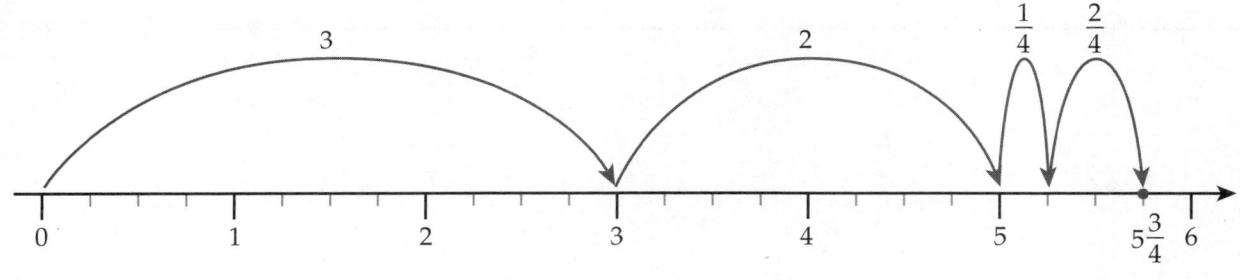

$$3 + 2 + \frac{1}{4} + \frac{2}{4} = 5\frac{3}{4}$$

So, $3\frac{1}{4} + 2\frac{2}{4} = 5\frac{3}{4}$.

FRACTIONS AND DECIMALS

18 Adding Mixed Numbers with Like Denominators

Anna uses this method to add $3\frac{1}{4} + 2\frac{2}{4}$.

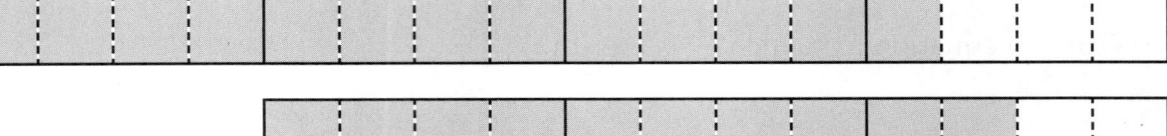

Add the whole-number parts.

$$3 + 2 = 5$$

Add the fraction parts.

$$\frac{1}{4} + \frac{2}{4} = \frac{3}{4}$$

Combine them.

$$5 + \frac{3}{4} = 5\frac{3}{4}$$

$$\text{So, } 3\frac{1}{4} + 2\frac{2}{4} = 5\frac{3}{4}$$

Adding Mixed Numbers with Like Denominators 18

Tamika uses this method to add $3\frac{1}{4} + 2\frac{2}{4}$.

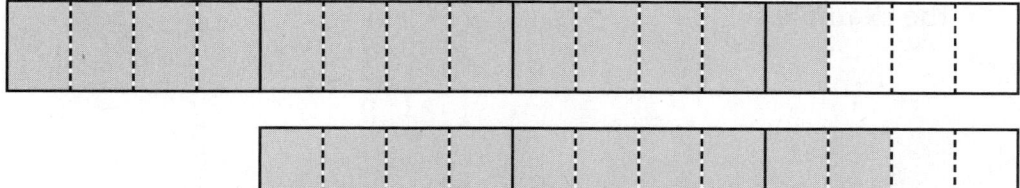

Write each mixed number as an improper fraction.

$$3\frac{1}{4} = \frac{4}{4} + \frac{4}{4} + \frac{4}{4} + \frac{1}{4} = \frac{13}{4}$$

$$2\frac{2}{4} = \frac{4}{4} + \frac{4}{4} + \frac{2}{4} = \frac{10}{4}$$

Add the improper fractions.

$$\frac{13}{4} + \frac{10}{4} = \frac{23}{4}$$

Write the improper fraction as a mixed number.

$$\frac{23}{4} = 5\frac{3}{4}$$

So, $3\frac{1}{4} + 2\frac{2}{4} = 5\frac{3}{4}$

18 Adding Mixed Numbers with Like Denominators

➔ work time

1. Find the sum. Write your answer as an equation. Use one of the methods shown in the examples.

$$2\frac{1}{6} + 2\frac{2}{6}$$

2. Find the sum. Write your answer as an equation. Use a method different from the one you used in problem 1.

$$3\frac{5}{8} + 1\frac{2}{8}$$

Adding Mixed Numbers with Like Denominators 18

3. Find the sum. Write your answer as an equation. Use a method different from the one you used in problems 1 and 2.

$$1\frac{1}{10} + 2\frac{6}{10}$$

18 Adding Mixed Numbers with Like Denominators

4. Josh said that $1\frac{1}{3} + 2\frac{2}{3} = 3\frac{3}{6}$. Josh is incorrect. Explain what Josh did wrong. Fix his mistake. What advice would you give Josh?

reflection

I think adding mixed numbers is   easy   difficult   (circle one) because…

Subtracting Mixed Numbers with Like Denominators

⊃ show me

Write the subtraction equation that matches the tape diagram.

⊃ setting the direction

A bucket has $2\frac{8}{10}$ gallons of water in it. Josh, Maria, and Anthony pour out $1\frac{3}{10}$ gallons of water. How many gallons of water are left in the bucket?

Josh, Maria, and Anthony each used a different method to solve this problem.

Name: __Josh__

1. A bucket has $2\frac{8}{10}$ gallons of water in it. Josh, Maria, and Anthony pour out $1\frac{3}{10}$ gallons of water. How many gallons of water are left in the bucket?

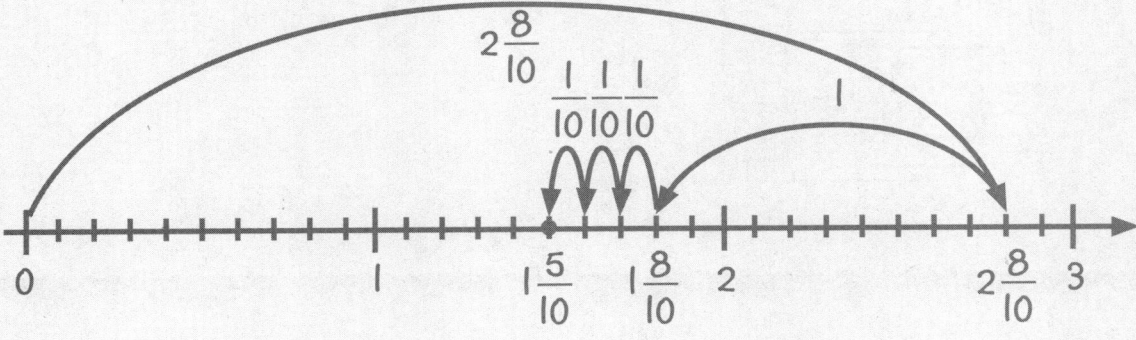

$2\frac{8}{10} - 1\frac{3}{10} = 1\frac{5}{10}$

FRACTIONS AND DECIMALS

19 Subtracting Mixed Numbers with Like Denominators

Name: __Maria__

1. A bucket has $2\frac{8}{10}$ gallons of water in it. Josh, Maria, and Anthony pour out $1\frac{3}{10}$ gallons of water. How many gallons of water are left in the bucket?

$2\frac{8}{10} - 1\frac{3}{10}$

$2\frac{8}{10} = \frac{10}{10} + \frac{10}{10} + \frac{8}{10} = \frac{28}{10}$

$1\frac{3}{10} = \frac{10}{10} + \frac{3}{10} = \frac{13}{10}$

$\frac{28}{10} - \frac{13}{10} = \frac{15}{10}$

$\frac{15}{10} = 1\frac{5}{10}$

Name: __Anthony__

1. A bucket has $2\frac{8}{10}$ gallons of water in it. Josh, Maria, and Anthony pour out $1\frac{3}{10}$ gallons of water. How many gallons of water are left in the bucket?

$2\frac{8}{10} - 1\frac{3}{10} = 1\frac{5}{10}$

Josh, Maria, and Anthony said:

> "We show the same answer."

They wrote an equation to show their work.

$2\frac{8}{10} - 1\frac{3}{10} = 1\frac{5}{10}$

Josh said:

> "There are $1\frac{5}{10}$ gallons of water left in the bucket."

19 Subtracting Mixed Numbers with Like Denominators

work time

1. A hardware store keeps track of how much rope it sells every day.

   The table on page 105 shows how much rope was in stock at the start of the day and how much rope was sold that day.

   Complete the table.

   - Subtract the amount sold from the amount in stock.
   - Use a method shown in the examples. Show your work on page 106.
   - Write the difference in the "Amount Remaining" column.
   - If the amount remaining is less than 3 yards, check the "Need to Order" column.
   - For one type of rope, there is a mistake in the amount of rope sold. Circle that row. Explain the mistake.

Subtracting Mixed Numbers with Like Denominators — 19

Rope Type	Amount in Stock (in yards)	Amount Sold (in yards)	Amount Remaining (in yards)	Need to Order
$\frac{1}{2}$-inch manila rope	$8\frac{5}{6}$	$7\frac{3}{6}$	$8\frac{5}{6} - 7\frac{3}{6} = 1\frac{2}{6}$	✓
$\frac{1}{4}$-inch braided nylon rope	$9\frac{2}{3}$	$7\frac{1}{3}$		
$\frac{3}{8}$-inch polyester rope	$4\frac{1}{2}$	1		
$\frac{3}{4}$-inch twisted polyester rope	$7\frac{3}{6}$	$9\frac{4}{6}$		
$\frac{5}{8}$-inch multicolored rope	$8\frac{3}{4}$	$3\frac{1}{4}$		
$\frac{1}{8}$-inch vinyl-coated rope	$5\frac{5}{8}$	$3\frac{2}{8}$		

19 Subtracting Mixed Numbers with Like Denominators

Show your work here.

reflection

I think that subtracting mixed numbers is   easy   difficult   (circle one)
because…

Adding and Subtracting Mixed Numbers with Unlike Denominators

20

⟳ setting the direction

Use an area model to show the calculation below, then give the answer in simplest form.

$$\frac{1}{6} + \frac{2}{3} =$$

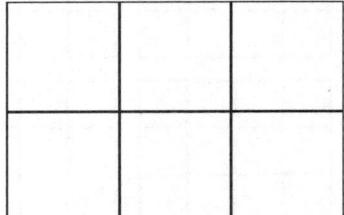

Use a number line to show the calculation below, then give the answer in simplest form.

$$\frac{11}{12} - \frac{1}{4} =$$

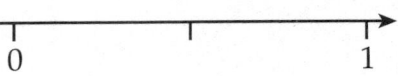

20 Adding and Subtracting Mixed Numbers with Unlike Denominators

work time

Complete these calculations. Problem 1 is partially done as an example. Simplify your final answer to lowest terms.

	Calculation	Diagram	Other True Statements
1.	$1\frac{1}{4} + 1\frac{2}{3} =$ $\frac{}{12} + \frac{}{12} =$ $2\frac{}{12}$		$1\frac{2}{3} + 1\frac{1}{4} = 2\frac{}{12}$ $2\frac{}{12} - 1\frac{2}{3} = 1\frac{1}{4}$ $2\frac{}{12} - 1\frac{1}{4} = 1\frac{2}{3}$
2.	$1\frac{5}{6} + \frac{1}{2} =$		
3.	$1\frac{3}{8} + \frac{3}{4} =$		

Adding and Subtracting Mixed Numbers with Unlike Denominators 20

Calculation	Diagram	Other True Statements
4. $1\frac{1}{8} - \frac{3}{4} =$		
5. $1\frac{3}{4} + 1\frac{2}{3} =$		
6. $3\frac{7}{8} - 1\frac{3}{4} =$		
7. $2\frac{1}{3} - 1\frac{3}{4} =$		

FRACTIONS AND DECIMALS

20 Adding and Subtracting Mixed Numbers with Unlike Denominators

Calculation	Diagram	Other True Statements
8. Make up your own.		

9. Look back at your work in problems 1–8. Describe a process that you could use to add or subtract mixed numbers if you did not want to use a diagram.

10. How is your process like the process that you use to add or subtract proper fractions? How is it different?

⟶ show me

Show me an addition problem using mixed numbers that has a sum between 3 and 4. Solve your problem.

⟶ reflection

I am still confused about…

Multiplying Fractions by Whole Numbers

21

show me

Write $\frac{2}{3}$ as the product of a whole number and a unit fraction.

setting the direction

Anthony, Tamika, and Amir each used a different method to find $5 \times \frac{4}{6}$.

Name: __Anthony__

1. Find $5 \times \frac{4}{6}$. Show your work.

There are twenty $\frac{1}{6}$ parts shaded.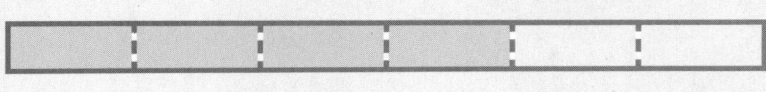

$5 \times \frac{4}{6} = \frac{20}{6}$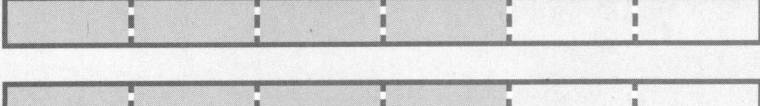

FRACTIONS AND DECIMALS | 115

21 Multiplying Fractions by Whole Numbers

Name: __Tamika__

1. Find $5 \times \frac{4}{6}$. Show your work.

$$5 \times \frac{4}{6} = \frac{4}{6} + \frac{4}{6} + \frac{4}{6} + \frac{4}{6} + \frac{4}{6} = \frac{5 \times 4}{6} = \frac{20}{6}$$

$$5 \times \frac{4}{6} = \frac{20}{6}$$

Name: __Amir__

1. Find $5 \times \frac{4}{6}$. Show your work.

$$\frac{4}{6} = 4 \times \frac{1}{6}$$

$$\text{So, } 5 \times \frac{4}{6} = 5 \times \left(4 \times \frac{1}{6}\right) = (5 \times 4) \times \frac{1}{6} = 20 \times \frac{1}{6} = \frac{20}{6}$$

$$5 \times \frac{4}{6} = \frac{20}{6}$$

⊃ work time

Use two of the ways shown in the examples to find each product. Show your work.

1. $3 \times \dfrac{3}{4}$

21 Multiplying Fractions by Whole Numbers

2. $4 \times \dfrac{7}{10}$

3. Tran says that when multiplying a fraction by a whole number, you can just multiply the whole number by the numerator and write the product over the denominator. Use two ways to show that Tran's answer is correct.

$$2 \times \frac{3}{8} = \frac{2 \times 3}{8} = \frac{6}{8}$$

21 Multiplying Fractions by Whole Numbers

reflection

The multiplication problems today were different from problems I have worked before because…

Multiplying Fractions — 22

⟳ setting the direction

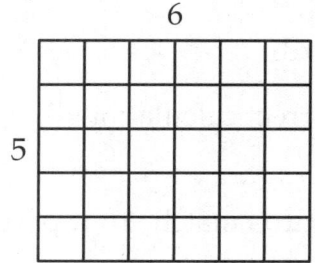

____ × ____ = ____

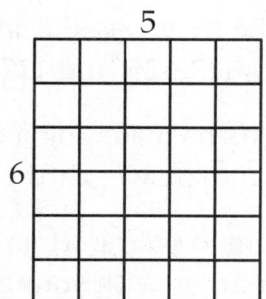

____ × ____ = ____

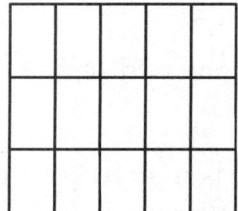

$\frac{3}{5}$ of $\frac{2}{3}$ =

$\frac{3}{5}$ of $\frac{2}{3}$ =

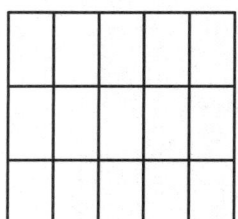

$\frac{2}{3}$ of $\frac{3}{5}$ =

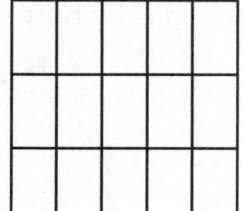

$\frac{2}{3}$ of $\frac{3}{5}$ =

22 Multiplying Fractions

work time

1. Work with a partner. You will need scissors and tape.

   - Get the *Diagrams*, *Calculations*, and *Answers* pages (pages 123, 125, and 127) and cut out all of the cards.

   - Take turns matching a diagram card with the correct calculation card and answer card.

   - Explain to your partner how you know that the cards match. Your partner should either agree with your explanation or challenge it.

   - When you and your partner agree, tape the matching cards together.

   - When you have matched all the cards, get the *Multiplication Problems* page (page 129) and cut out all of the cards.

   - Take turns matching the problem cards with your matched sets of diagrams and equations.

   - Explain to your partner how you know that the cards match. Your partner should either agree with your explanation or challenge it. When you and your partner agree, tape the matching cards together.

2. The product of two fractions is 1. What does this product tell you about the numerators and denominators of the fractions?

DIAGRAMS

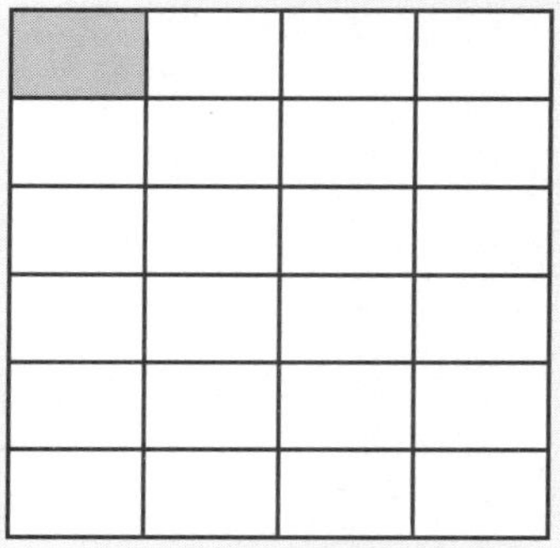

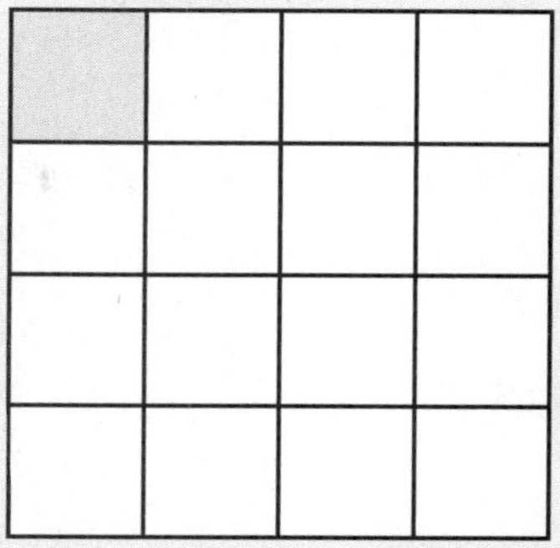

D1

D2

D3

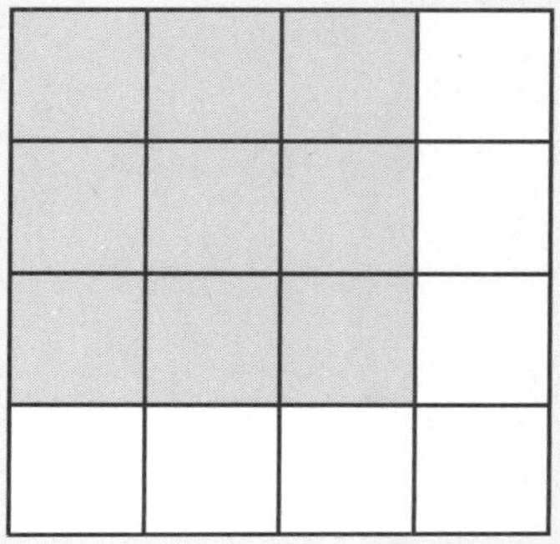

D4

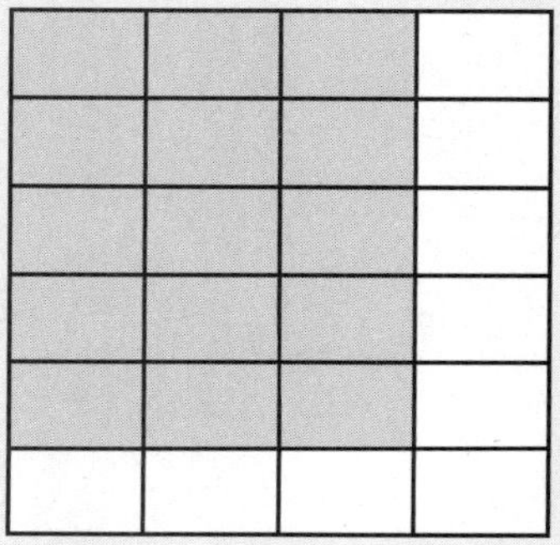

D5

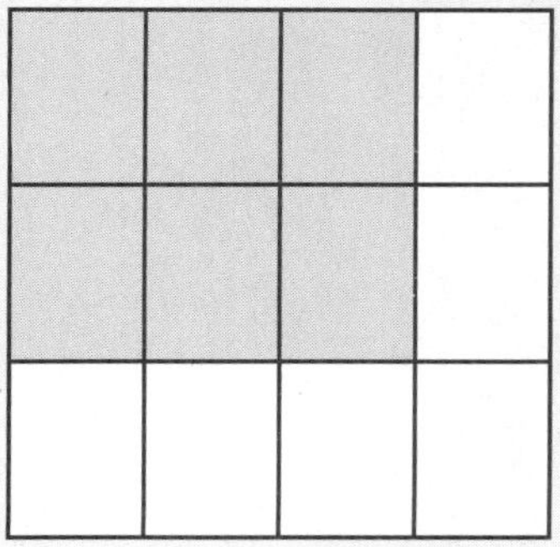

D6

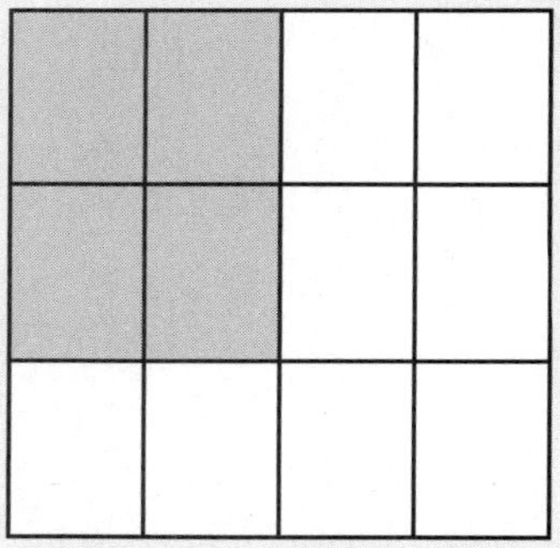

D7

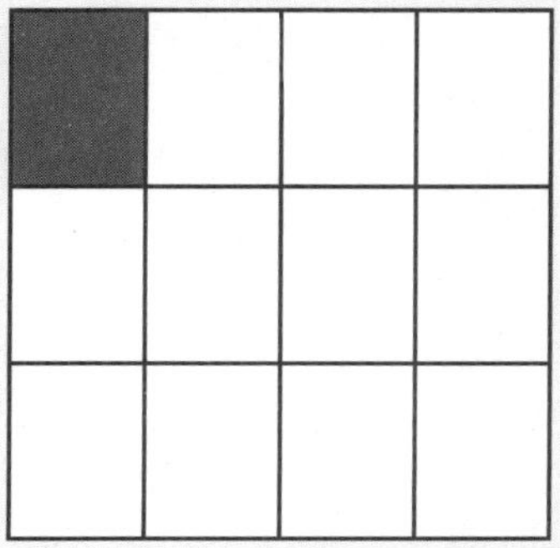

D8

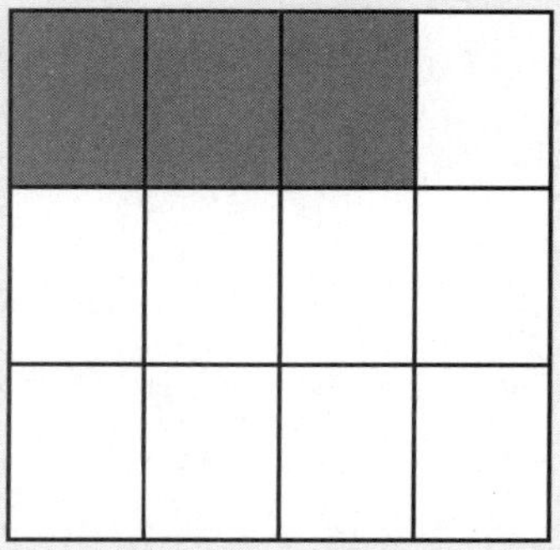

FRACTIONS AND DECIMALS

CALCULATIONS

C1
$$\frac{1}{4} \times \frac{1}{3} =$$

C2
$$\frac{3}{4} \times \frac{1}{3} =$$

C3
$$\frac{2}{3} \times \frac{1}{2} =$$

C4
$$\frac{3}{4} \times \frac{2}{3} =$$

C5
$$\frac{3}{4} \times \frac{3}{4} =$$

C6
$$\frac{1}{4} \times \frac{1}{4} =$$

C7
$$\frac{1}{4} \times \frac{1}{6} =$$

C8
$$\frac{5}{6} \times \frac{3}{4} =$$

ANSWERS

A1	A2
$\dfrac{1}{2}$	$\dfrac{1}{12}$

A3	A4
$\dfrac{1}{4}$	$\dfrac{1}{3}$

A5	A6
$\dfrac{9}{16}$	$\dfrac{1}{16}$

A7	A8
$\dfrac{1}{24}$	$\dfrac{5}{8}$

MULTIPLICATION PROBLEMS

P1

Josh's family ate $\frac{2}{3}$ of a cake while he was at basketball practice, leaving only $\frac{1}{3}$ of the cake. When Josh came home, he ate $\frac{1}{4}$ of the cake that was left. How much of the whole cake did he eat?

P2

Anna mowed $\frac{2}{3}$ of the lawn before lunch. After lunch, she mowed $\frac{3}{4}$ of what was left before it started to rain. How much of the lawn did she mow after finishing her lunch?

P3

One-half of the garden is planted with tomatoes. Gabby wants to use $\frac{2}{3}$ of the remaining space for beans. How much of the garden does Gabby want to use for beans?

P4

Amir's family wants to cover $\frac{2}{3}$ of the backyard with sod. But when the sod is delivered, there is only enough to complete $\frac{3}{4}$ of the job. How much of the backyard will his family be able to cover?

P5

Maria is good at shooting free throws during basketball games. She makes $\frac{3}{4}$ of the shots she attempts. If she takes 2 free throws, what is the chance that she will make both of them?

P6

Tran had finished $\frac{1}{4}$ of his art project before he spilled paint on $\frac{1}{4}$ of what he had done. Now he has to re-do that part of the project! How much of the art project will he have to re-do?

P7

In the city park, $\frac{5}{6}$ of the area is covered with grass. One-fourth of the remaining area is used for a playground for young children. How much of the park is used for the playground?

P8

Three-fourths of the pool is considered to be deep water. Approximately $\frac{5}{6}$ of the deep water is deep enough for diving. About how much of the pool is deep enough for diving?

FRACTIONS AND DECIMALS

show me

Show me at least two fractions whose product is $\frac{1}{12}$.

reflection

I am still having trouble with…

Dividing Unit Fractions   23

⊃ show me

Show me a number line or a tape diagram divided into 5 equal parts. Then, divide each of those parts into 2 equal parts. What fraction does each part of your diagram show now?

⊃ work time

Fill in the missing parts of each table.

Problem
1. Tran has $\frac{1}{3}$ of a large tub of popcorn to share with a friend. How much of the tub will each of the 2 boys get?

Diagram	Calculation
Words	Answer

FRACTIONS AND DECIMALS

23 Dividing Unit Fractions

Problem
2. The community pool sponsors a Fitness Day every year. One of the activities is a $\frac{1}{2}$-mile team relay race. If each team consists of 4 swimmers, and each teammate swims 1 equal part of the distance of the race, how far will each teammate swim?

Diagram	Calculation
	|//
Words	**Answer**
A $\frac{1}{2}$-mile length is divided into 4 equal parts.	

Problem
3. Mrs. Chi ordered $\frac{1}{5}$ ton of mulch for her yard. She uses an equal amount of mulch in each of her 3 flower beds. How much mulch will she put in each flower bed?

Diagram	Calculation
3 flowerbeds — $\frac{1}{5}$ of a ton	
Words	**Answer**

FRACTIONS AND DECIMALS

Dividing Unit Fractions — 23

Problem	
4.	

Diagram	Calculation
	$\frac{1}{6} \div 2$
Words	**Answer**

5. a. How are these problems like dividing whole numbers?

   b. How are they different?

23 Dividing Unit Fractions

reflection

It makes sense to talk about half of a ... (List some examples.)

- mile
-
-
-

It does *not* make sense to talk about half of a ... (List some examples.)

- person
-
-
-

Dividing by Unit Fractions

setting the direction

Solve the following equations.

Hint: You can write the calculation in words and draw a diagram.

$\dfrac{1}{3} \div 2 = \boxed{}$ $\dfrac{1}{2} \div 4 = \boxed{}$ $\dfrac{1}{6} \div 2 = \boxed{}$ $\dfrac{1}{4} \div 5 = \boxed{}$ $\dfrac{1}{5} \div 3 = \boxed{}$

work time

1. Work with a partner.

   - Complete the table on the next page.

   - Using the diagrams, take turns solving the division equations.

   - It may help you to rewrite the problem as a multiplication problem. Write your equation in the space to the right of the number line, as shown in part a.

   - In the last two problems, complete the diagrams first.

   - Make sure to justify your answers to your partner. Your partner should either agree with your explanation or challenge it if it is not clear and complete.

24 Dividing by Unit Fractions

a. $2 \div \frac{1}{6} =$ 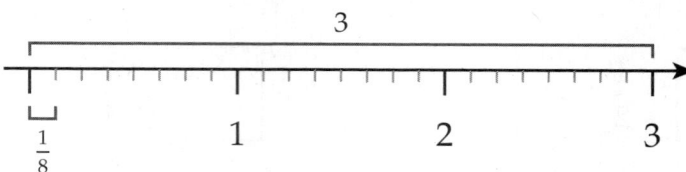 $\frac{1}{6} \times \boxed{} = 2$

b. $3 \div \frac{1}{8} =$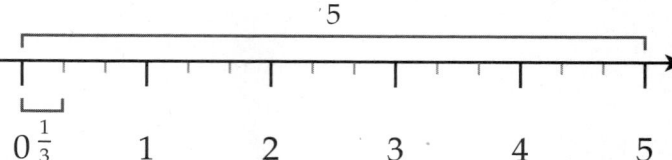

c. $5 \div \frac{1}{3} =$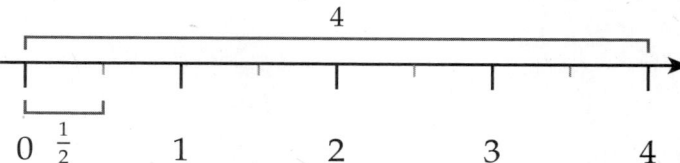

d. $4 \div \frac{1}{2} =$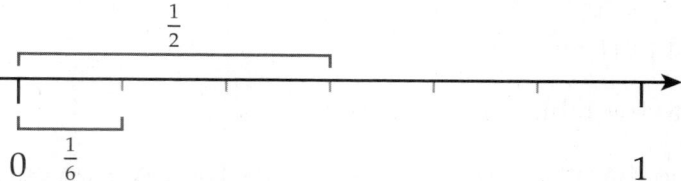

e. $\frac{1}{2} \div \frac{1}{6} =$

f. $3 \div \frac{1}{4} =$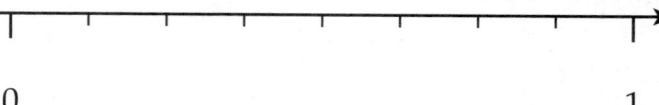

g. $\frac{3}{4} \div \frac{1}{8} =$

2. How do you divide fractions when the dividend is a whole number and the divisor is a unit fraction?

show me

Show me a number line that goes from 0 to 5 and that is divided into lengths of $\frac{1}{5}$ unit. How many $\frac{1}{5}$-unit lengths did you make?

reflection

Dividing by unit fractions is easier if you …

Fraction Operations Word Problems

25

⟶ setting the direction

A water tank is filled at a rate of $\frac{1}{2}$ gallon per second.

- After 5 seconds, how much water is in the tank?
- After $\frac{1}{4}$ second, how much water is in the tank?
- If the tank contains 1 gallon, how much time has passed?
- If the tank contains 100 gallons, how much time has passed?
- If the tank contains $\frac{1}{4}$ gallon, how much time has passed?

⟶ work time

Sketch a diagram and show calculations to solve each problem. Compare your diagrams and calculations with a partner and take turns explaining why each approach works.

If your approach does not work, work together to modify your diagram and calculation as needed to solve the problem correctly.

1. A trencher can dig $\frac{2}{3}$ of a mile in a day. How much can it dig in $\frac{4}{5}$ of a day?

FRACTIONS AND DECIMALS

2. A water tank that holds 60 gallons is filled at a rate of $\frac{4}{5}$ of a gallon per second. How long does it take to fill the tank to $\frac{2}{3}$ of its capacity?

3. A stack of 500 sheets of paper is 2 inches tall. How many sheets are in a stack $\frac{3}{4}$ inch tall?

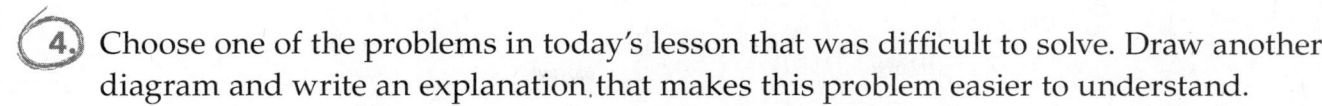

4. Choose one of the problems in today's lesson that was difficult to solve. Draw another diagram and write an explanation that makes this problem easier to understand.

show me

Show me the product: $\frac{1}{8} \times 2$

reflection

One thing I know about multiplying with fractions is…

Representing Tenths and Hundredths

show me

Show me this amount in at least two different ways. (■ = 1 unit)

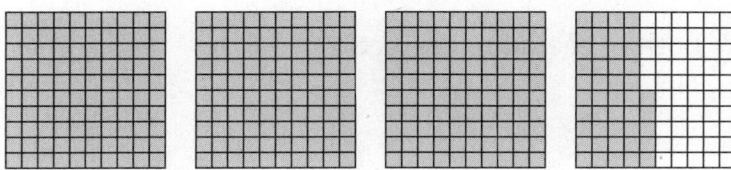

work time

1. Explain why $\frac{3}{10} = \frac{30}{100}$.

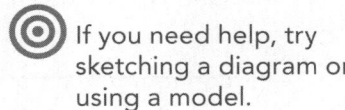 If you need help, try sketching a diagram or using a model.

26 Representing Tenths and Hundredths

2. Miguel said that the point marked below is one and four-tenths. Gabby said that it is one and forty hundredths.

Explain why both of them are correct.

3. a. Use fractions or mixed numbers to name point A in at least two ways.

b. Explain why you think both names are names for point A.

c. On the number line above, mark the point $3\frac{4}{10}$ using the letter B.

d. What other names can you use for point *B*?

4. Anthony did his homework too quickly. He got some problems wrong. Correct Anthony's mistakes below.

   Name: __Anthony__

   a. $0.9 = \dfrac{9}{100}$

   b. $\dfrac{250}{100} = 2.5$

   c. $\dfrac{7}{10} = 0.07$

   d. $0.80 = 8.0$

reflection

Three (or more) things I know about tenths and hundredths are…

Decimals and the Zero

setting the direction

Find the number you need to subtract.

5,981 – _____ = 5,081

18,398 – _____ = 18,308

9,576 – _____ = 576

1.59 – _____ = 1.5

1.95 – _____ = 1.05

1.95 – _____ = 1.5

27 Decimals and the Zero

work time

1. Work with a partner. You will need scissors, tape, poster paper, and a calculator.

   - Get page 151, *Always True or Sometimes True?*, and cut out all of the cards.

   - Divide your poster paper into two columns. Label the columns "Always True" and "Sometimes True."

   - Take turns placing a card in one of the columns.

   - Explain your reasons for choosing that column to your partner. Your partner should agree with your explanation or challenge it, if it is not clear, correct, and complete.

   - When you both agree that the card is placed correctly, tape the card to the poster.

   - Next to each card, write how you know the statement is always true or sometimes true, and give an example or a counterexample.

2. Change one of the "Sometimes True" statements to make it always true.

show me

Show me two decimals that result in a number with 0 in the tenths place when they are subtracted.

reflection

I think zero matters when...

ALWAYS TRUE OR SOMETIMES TRUE?

A
If you put a 0 at the left end of a number, the size of the number does not change.

2.6 → 02.6

B
If you put a 0 in the middle of a number, the size of the number changes.

54 → 504

C
If you put a 0 at the right end of a number, the size of the number changes.

5 → 50

D
If you put a 0 at the right end of a decimal measurement, it means the measurement is more accurate.

2.6 m and 2.60 m

E
When you multiply a number by 10, you put a 0 at the right end of the number.

60 × 10 = 600

F
When you divide a decimal number by 10, you put a 0 just after the decimal point.

0.4 ÷ 10 = 0.04

G
When you type a number into a calculator and press =, the 0s at the beginning and end all disappear.

00080.304000

H
When you change a fraction with a denominator of a power of ten to a decimal, you get the same number of decimal places in the decimal as you have 0s in the fraction.

$$\frac{1}{100} = 0.01$$

FRACTIONS AND DECIMALS

Powers of Ten — 28

> **setting the direction**

Move from number to number by writing the power of ten needed to multiply by or divide by.

You will also need to determine and write the proper multiplication (×) or division (÷) symbol when it is not provided.

The first step is already completed for you as an example.

759.3 ÷ [10] = 75.93 × [____] = 75,930

75,930 [__][____] = 759,300 [__][____] = 7,593

28 Powers of Ten

work time

1. a. Enter 1.23456 into your calculator.

   b. Change it to the next number (12.3456) in the diagram below by multiplying. Write the power of ten you used in the boxes.

   c. Continue across the first row by multiplying or dividing. Enter all the factors, divisors, and operations you use. When you reach the end of a row, continue at the start of the next row until you reach the end.

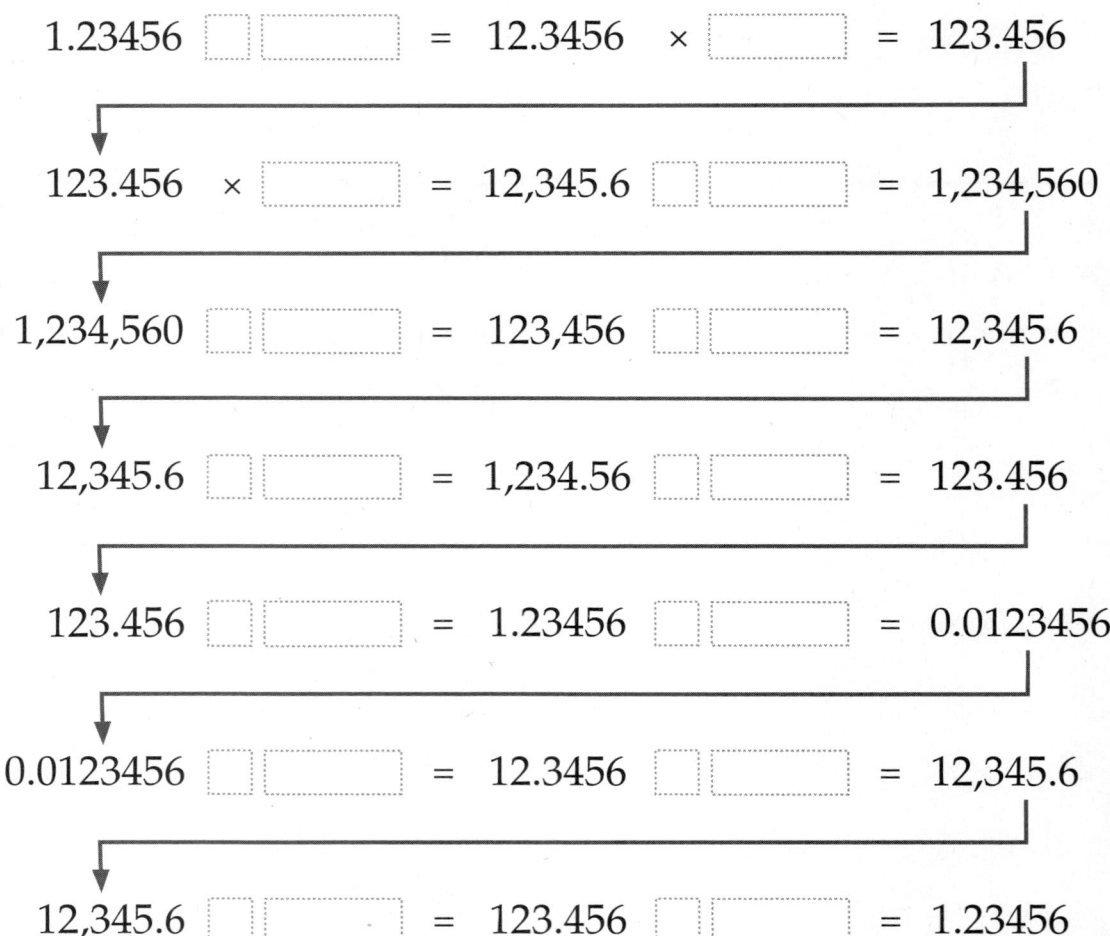

2. Now work alone to create your own puzzle.

   - Write a decimal number on the first line of the first row in the answer key below.

   - Write an operation (× or ÷) and a power of ten in the next two boxes to the right. Calculate the result and write it on the next line to the right. When you get to the end of a row, copy the result on the last line of that row to the first line of the next row. Repeat this process until you reach the last line of the last row.

   - Based on your work below, create a puzzle on page 157, *Powers of Ten Puzzle*.

   - Get page 157, write your name as "Puzzle maker," and give it to your partner to solve. Write your name as "Puzzle solver" on the sheet your partner gives to you.

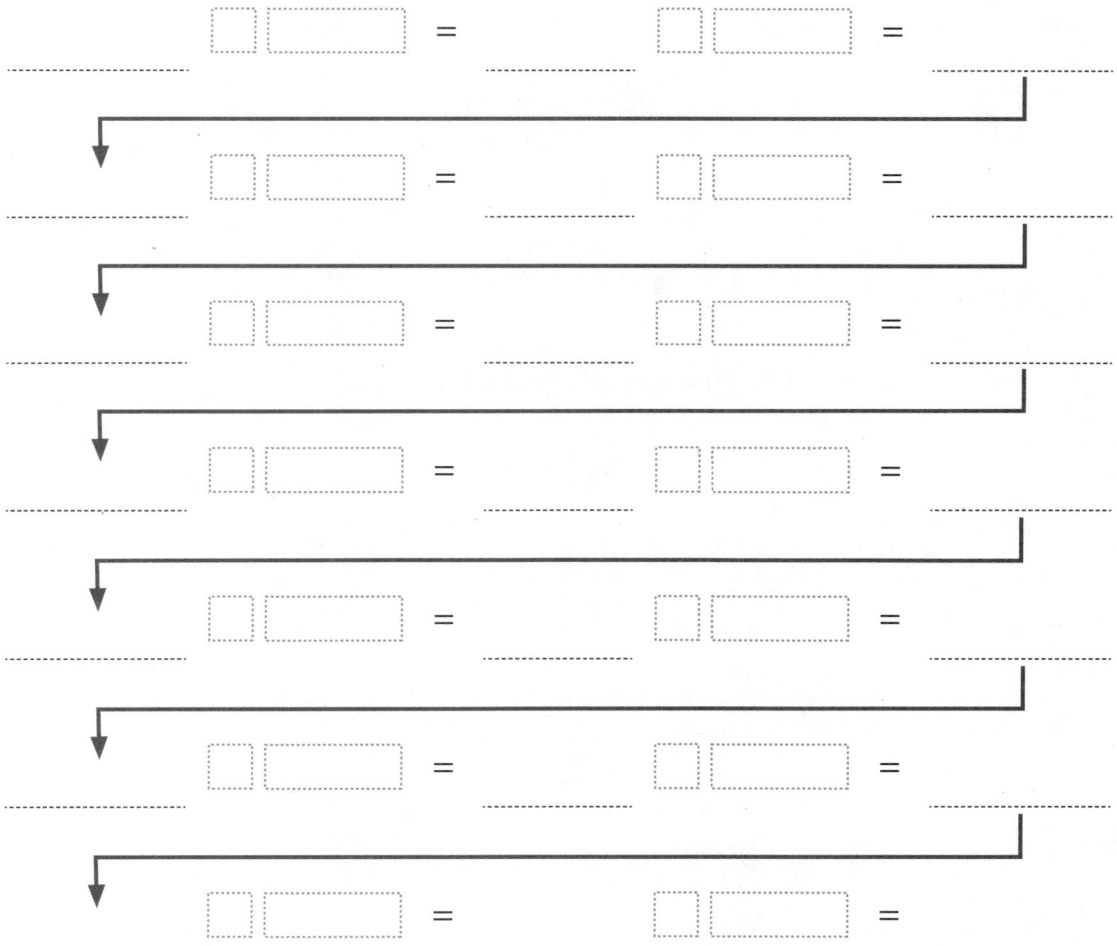

28 Powers of Ten

3. What patterns have you noticed about multiplying and dividing decimals by powers of ten?

show me

Show me a way to multiply or divide with powers of ten so that you end up with the number you started with.

reflection

The most difficult part in creating the problem was…

POWERS OF TEN PUZZLE

Puzzle maker: _____ **Puzzle solver:** _____

Equivalent Decimals and Fractions

show me

Show me the number $5\frac{2}{10}$ using fractions, mixed numbers or decimals, in as many ways as you can.

work time

1. Work with your partner.

   - Get page 163, *Fraction and Decimal Cards*, and cut out all the cards.

   - Take out blank cards. Mix up the remaining cards and lay them facedown so both you and your partner can see every card.

   - Choose two cards and turn them faceup. Allow time for both you and your partner to look at the cards.

   - If both you and your partner agree that the cards represent equivalent fractions, keep both cards and record the match in your student pages. Otherwise, turn the cards facedown again in the same spots.

   - Then your partner takes a turn doing the same thing, keeping both cards if they represent equivalent fractions and recording the match.

   - The game ends when all the cards are claimed.

   - The winner is the partner who has the most cards at the end.

29 Equivalent Decimals and Fractions

Record your matched cards below.

My Matches		
=	=	=
=	=	=
=	=	=
=	=	=
=	=	=

2. Which cards were the hardest for you? What made them hard?

29 Equivalent Decimals and Fractions

⟶ reflection

I like (circle one)   fractions   decimals   best because…

FRACTION AND DECIMAL CARDS

0.05	$\frac{5}{10}$	33.10	$\frac{33}{100}$
6.2	$6\frac{1}{2}$	2.4	$2\frac{1}{4}$
$6\frac{10}{20}$	$2\frac{40}{100}$	$\frac{5}{100}$	6.20
0.33	$\frac{33}{10}$	$\frac{50}{100}$	5.10
$33\frac{1}{10}$	$2\frac{25}{100}$	5.1	$3\frac{3}{10}$

Comparing Decimals

⊃ setting the direction

Write these decimals in order from least (smallest) to greatest (largest):

0.75   0.4   0.375   0.25   0.125   0.04   0.8

Describe your method for ordering the numbers.

30 Comparing Decimals

work time

1. Work with a partner. You will need scissors and tape.

   - Get the *Decimal Cards*, *Area Cards*, and *Number Line Cards* pages (pages 167, 169, and 171).

   - Cut out all of the cards.

   - Take turns with your partner matching a decimal card with an area card and a number line card.

   - When you make a match, explain to your partner how you know that those cards make a set.

   - Your partner should either agree with your explanation or challenge it if your explanation is not clear, correct, and complete.

   - When you agree, tape the three matching cards together.

   - Create your own set of cards that have a matching decimal, area model, and number line using the blank cards **H**, **8**, and **HH**.

   - When you are done matching all the cards and creating your own set, place the sets of cards in order from least to greatest.

2. Jong says he can write the decimal 0.12 as $\frac{1}{10} + \frac{2}{100}$. Marita says that she can write 0.12 as $\frac{12}{100}$. Which student is correct? Explain why.

166 FRACTIONS AND DECIMALS

DECIMAL CARDS

A 0.8	**B** 0.04
C 0.25	**D** 0.375
E 0.4	**F** 0.125
G 0.75	**H**

AREA CARDS

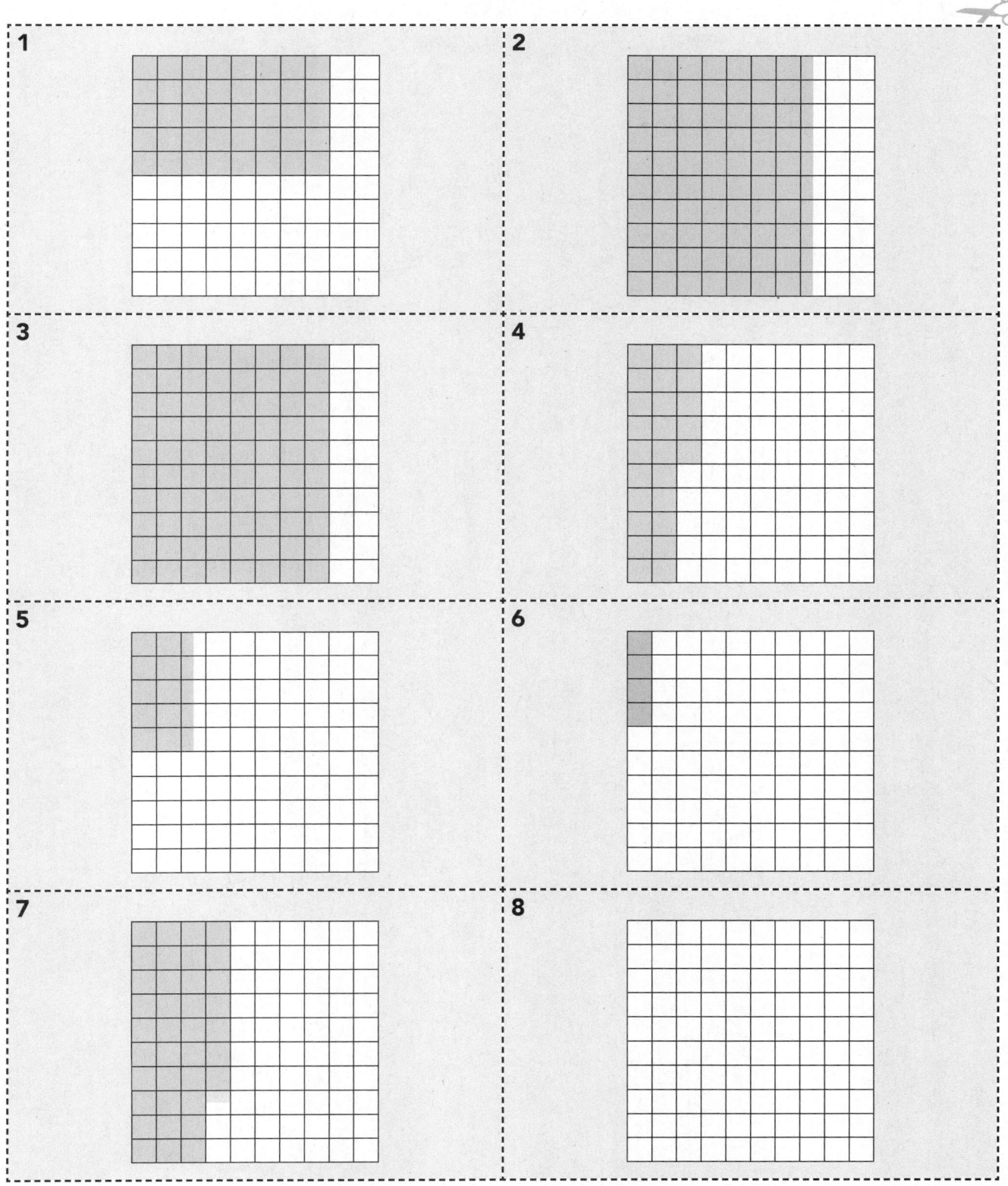

NUMBER LINE CARDS

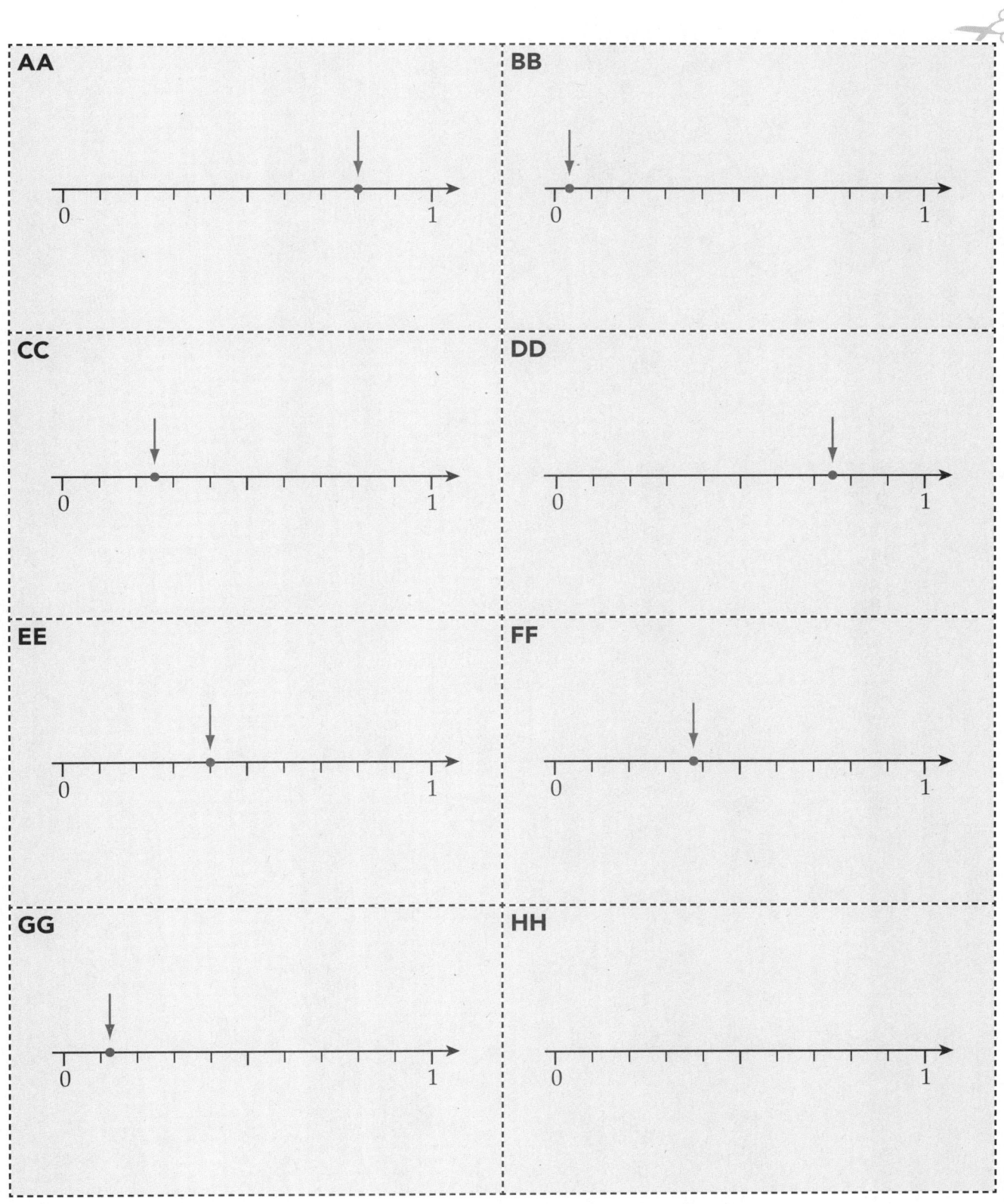

show me

Show me two decimals, one of which is 0.375 greater than the other.

reflection

I cannot use the number of digits in decimals to compare their values because …

Ordering Decimals

setting the direction

Here is a list of results from a women's 100-meter race.

Women's 100-Meter Race

Competitor	Time (seconds)
Angela	12.2
Bettina	12
Carla	12.15
Dolores	11.76
Eiko	11.6
Faith	12.08
Gabby	12.35
Hannah	11.9

Write the results in order of finish, winner first (from shortest time to longest time). Use the number line below if you need help.

Competitor	Time (seconds)

◎ Check your answers using the number line below.

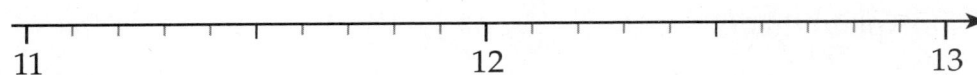

FRACTIONS AND DECIMALS — 175

31 Ordering Decimals

work time

1. a. Work with a partner to put the women's high jump competitors in order, winner first.

   In this event the winner has the highest jump, so the order is highest to lowest (greatest to least).

   First try to determine the order by examining the numbers. Write your results in the "Without the Number Line" column below.

Women's High Jump	
Angela	1.95 meters
Jin	1.9 meters
Marita	1.84 meters
Natalia	1.88 meters
Rosa	1.81 meters
Sarah	1.8 meters
Tamika	1.94 meters

Women's High Jump	Without the Number Line		Using the Number Line	
	Name	Height	Name	Height
1st place				
2nd place				
3rd place				
4th place				
5th place				
6th place				
7th place				

Check your ordering using the number line; then write the names and heights in the "Using the Number Line" column above.

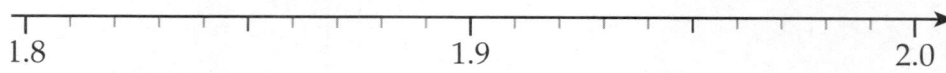

b. Compare your "Without" and "Using the Number Line" columns. Are there any differences? If so, explain them.

Ordering Decimals 31

2. a. Work with a partner to put the men's 100-meter race competitors in order, winner first (shortest time to longest time).

   First try to determine the order by examining the numbers. Write your results in the "Without the Number Line" column below.

Men's 100-Meter Race	
Andy	10.9 seconds
Boris	10.23 seconds
Claude	10.64 seconds
Jong	10.03 seconds
Misha	10.4 seconds
Pablo	10.19 seconds
Tran	10.69 seconds

Men's 100-Meter Race	Without the Number Line		Using the Number Line	
	Name	Time	Name	Time
1st place				
2nd place				
3rd place				
4th place				
5th place				
6th place				
7th place				

◎ Check your ordering using the number line, and write your results in the "Using the Number Line" column above.

10.0　　　　　　　10.5　　　　　　　11.0

b. Compare your "Without" and "Using the Number Line" columns. Are there any differences? If so, explain them.

31 Ordering Decimals

3. a. What kinds of mistakes did you make in ordering the results?

   b. What do you understand now that will help you avoid these mistakes?

show me

Show me a number to three decimal places that is less than 10.0001 but more than 9.9999.

reflection

The number lines help me order decimals because...

Estimating Decimal Operations

32

⮕ setting the direction

Target Number Game Instructions for 100

You need two players and one calculator. To play:

- Player A enters any number into the calculator.

- Player B then has to multiply this number by another number so that the answer will be as close to the target number (100) as possible.

- Player A then multiplies this new answer by a number, trying to get nearer still to 100.

- Players take turns until one player reaches the target by getting 100.******* (100 followed by any decimal digits on the calculator display.)

Here is a sample game:

example

Target Number: 100

Player	Keys Pressed	Display	Thoughts
A	64	64	
B	× 1.5	96	Hmm... a bit small!
A	× 1.2	115.2	Oh... it is off by about 15.
B	× 0.9	103.68	Nearly! Only 3 too much.
A	× 0.9	93.312	I keep missing... about 7 too low.
B	× 1.08	100.77696	I win!

FRACTIONS AND DECIMALS — 179

32 Estimating Decimal Operations

Record the whole class game in the chart below.

Target Number: 100

Player	Keys Pressed	Display

work time

1. Play the Target Number Game with your partner. You will need a calculator.

    - Get the *Target Number Game* record sheet pages (pages 183 and 184).
    - For each game you play, fill in the target number given.
    - Use only the specified operation (multiplication or division) on your calculator to get as close to the target number as you can.

    a. **Target 100: Multiplication**

    Play the Target Number Game with your partner using only multiplication on your calculator. Get as close to the target number of 100 as you can.

    b. **Target 100: Division**

    Play the Target Number Game with your partner using only division on your calculator. Get as close to the target number of 100 as you can.

    c. **Target 1: Multiplication**

    Play the Target Number Game with your partner using only multiplication on your calculator. Get as close to the target number of 1 as you can.

2. If you multiply a number by a number less than 1, is your answer smaller or larger than the original number? Explain why.

32 Estimating Decimal Operations

3. If you divide a number by a number less than 1, is your answer smaller or larger than the original number? Explain why.

4. Say why a game like the ones in this lesson called "Target 1: Division" would be a boring game.

show me

Show me the symbol (>, <, or =) that fills in the blank:

1.5 × 10 _____ 15

reflection

Some strategies I used to play the Target Number Game were...

TARGET NUMBER GAME

Target Number: _____

Player	Keys Pressed	Display

Target Number: _____

Player	Keys Pressed	Display

TARGET NUMBER GAME

Target Number: _____

Player	Keys Pressed	Display

Target Number: _____

Player	Keys Pressed	Display

Decimal Sequences 33

setting the direction

Rosa wants to buy some crackers that cost $1.20 from a vending machine. The "exact change" light is on. She does not have any dollars, but she has quarters, dimes, and nickels.

Can she pay exactly $1.20 using *only one* kind of coin in the machine?

The machine shows a new total after each coin is put in. Use the tables below to show what Rosa will need to put in the machine to buy the crackers. (To save space, some rows are not shown.)

Quarters $0.25	Machine shows
1	0.25
2	0.50

Dimes $0.10	Machine shows
1	0.10
2	0.20
⋮	⋮
10	1.00

Nickels $0.05	Machine shows
1	0.05
⋮	⋮
10	0.50
⋮	⋮
20	1.00

FRACTIONS AND DECIMALS

33 Decimal Sequences

work time

Without using a calculator, continue each of these sequences.

example

Add on 0.35 each time.

0.35, 0.70, 1.05, 1.40, 1.75, 2.10, 2.45 ...

1. 0.2, 0.4, 0.6, _____ , _____ , _____ , _____ , _____

   (Add on 0.2 each time.)

2. 0.25, _____ , _____ , _____ , _____ , _____ , _____

   (Add on 0.25 each time.)

3. 0.05, _____ , _____ , _____ , _____ , _____ , _____ , _____

   (Add on 0.05 each time.)

FRACTIONS AND DECIMALS

Decimal Sequences 33

4. 0.15, _____ , _____ , _____ , _____ , _____ , _____ , _____

   (Add on 0.15 each time.)

5. 0.125, _____ , _____ , _____ , _____ , _____ , _____ , _____

   (Add on 0.125 each time.)

6. 6.4, 6.1, _____ , _____ , _____ , _____ , _____ , _____ , _____

   (Subtract 0.3 each time.)

7. 1.85, _____ , _____ , _____ , _____ , _____ , _____ , _____ , _____

   (Subtract 0.2 each time.)

8. 3.51, _____ , _____ , _____ , _____ , _____ , _____ , _____ , _____

   (Add on 0.1 each time.)

FRACTIONS AND DECIMALS

33 Decimal Sequences

work time check

Check your answers by skip-counting on the number line and by using a calculator (for example, press 0.35 + 0.35 = __ + 0.35 = __ …).

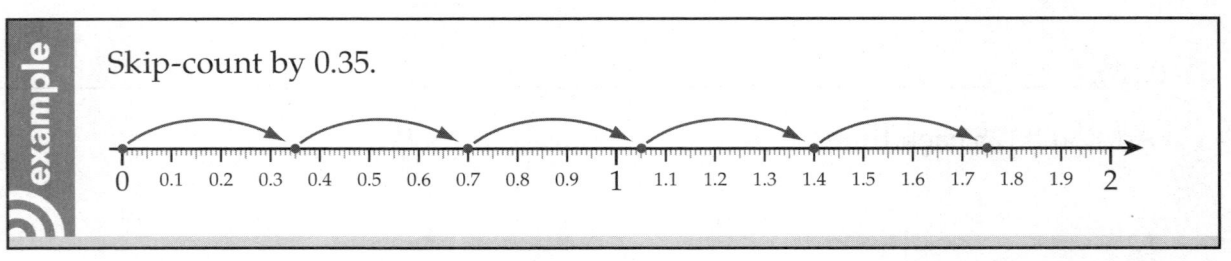

Skip-count by 0.35.

1. a. Skip-count by 0.2.

   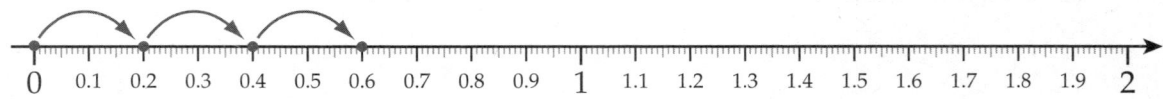

   b. Add on 0.2 using your calculator.

   0.2, 0.4, 0.6, _____ , _____ , _____ , _____ , _____

2. a. Skip-count by 0.25.

   b. Add on 0.25 using your calculator.

   0.25, _____ , _____ , _____ , _____ , _____ , _____

Decimal Sequences

3. a. Skip-count by 0.05.

   [number line from 0 to 2 marked in 0.1 increments]

   b. Add on 0.05 using your calculator.

   0.05, _____ , _____ , _____ , _____ , _____ , _____ , _____

4. a. Skip-count by 0.15.

   [number line from 0 to 2 marked in 0.1 increments]

   b. Add on 0.15 using your calculator.

   0.15, _____ , _____ , _____ , _____ , _____ , _____ , _____

5. a. Skip-count by 0.125.

   [number line from 0 to 2 marked in 0.1 increments]

   b. Add on 0.125 using your calculator.

   0.125, _____ , _____ , _____ , _____ , _____ , _____ , _____

33 Decimal Sequences

6. a. Skip-count down (subtract) by 0.3 from 6.4.

   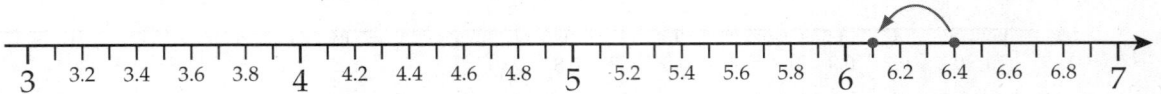

   b. Subtract 0.3 using your calculator.

   6.4, 6.1, _____, _____, _____, _____, _____, _____, _____, _____

7. a. Skip-count down by 0.2 from 1.85.

   b. Subtract 0.2 using your calculator.

   1.85, _____, _____, _____, _____, _____, _____, _____, _____

8. a. Skip-count by 0.1 from 3.51.

   b. Add on 0.1 using your calculator.

   3.51, _____, _____, _____, _____, _____, _____, _____, _____

FRACTIONS AND DECIMALS

Decimal Sequences

9. Write about any mistakes you made. How could you correct the mistakes?

show me

Show me a sequence of three numbers in which you skip-count by 0.3.

reflection

Using the number line helps me add decimals because…

Adding and Subtracting Decimals

→ **setting the direction**

Write the answers to the problems given by your teacher on your response board.

Use the number lines below.

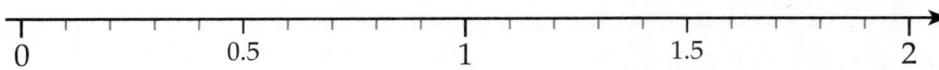

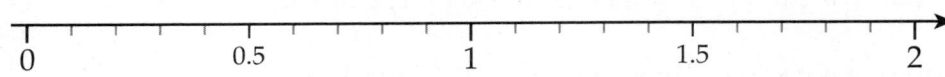

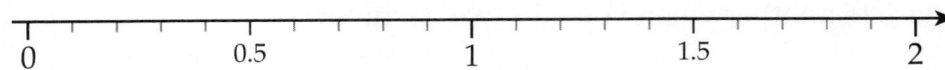

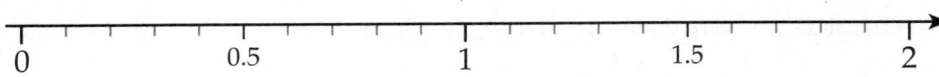

34 Adding and Subtracting Decimals

work time

1. Work with a partner. You will need scissors and tape.

   - Get *Hexagon Decimals*, pages 195, 197, and 199.

   - Cut out all of the triangles.

   - Take turns matching a calculation on one triangle with the correct answer on another triangle.

   - Explain to your partner how you know the calculation matches the answer. Your partner should either agree or challenge your explanation, if it is not clear, correct, and complete.

   - When you both agree, tape the matching edges of the triangles together.

   - Continue until all the pieces are together in one large hexagon.

   If you need help, use the number lines on page 201 to work out your calculations.

   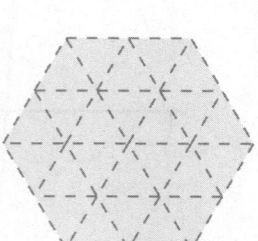

2. a. When doing column addition, what is the greatest digit that you could carry from one decimal place to another when you add two decimals?

   b. When doing column addition, what is the greatest digit that you could carry from one decimal place to another when you add three decimals?

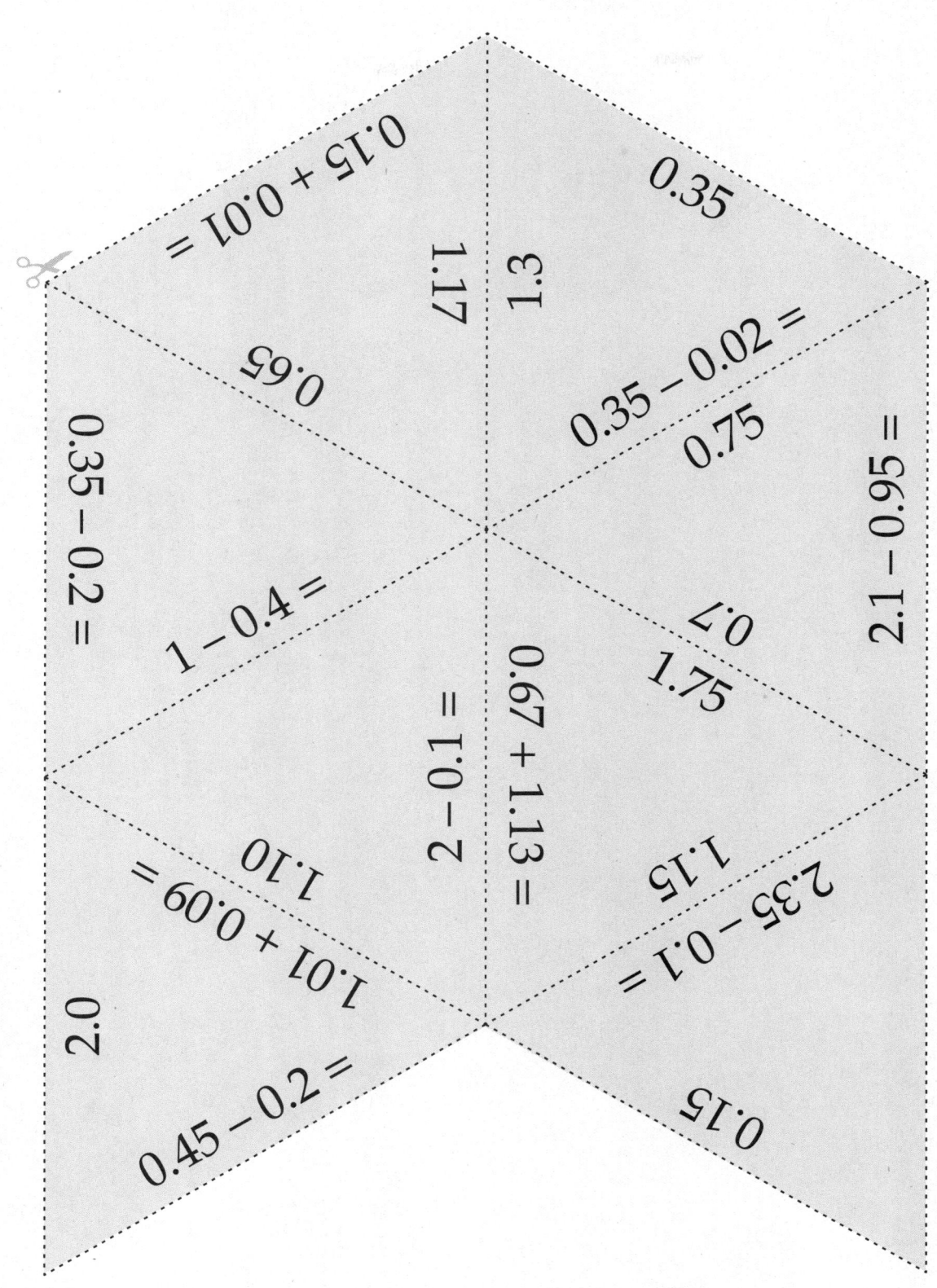

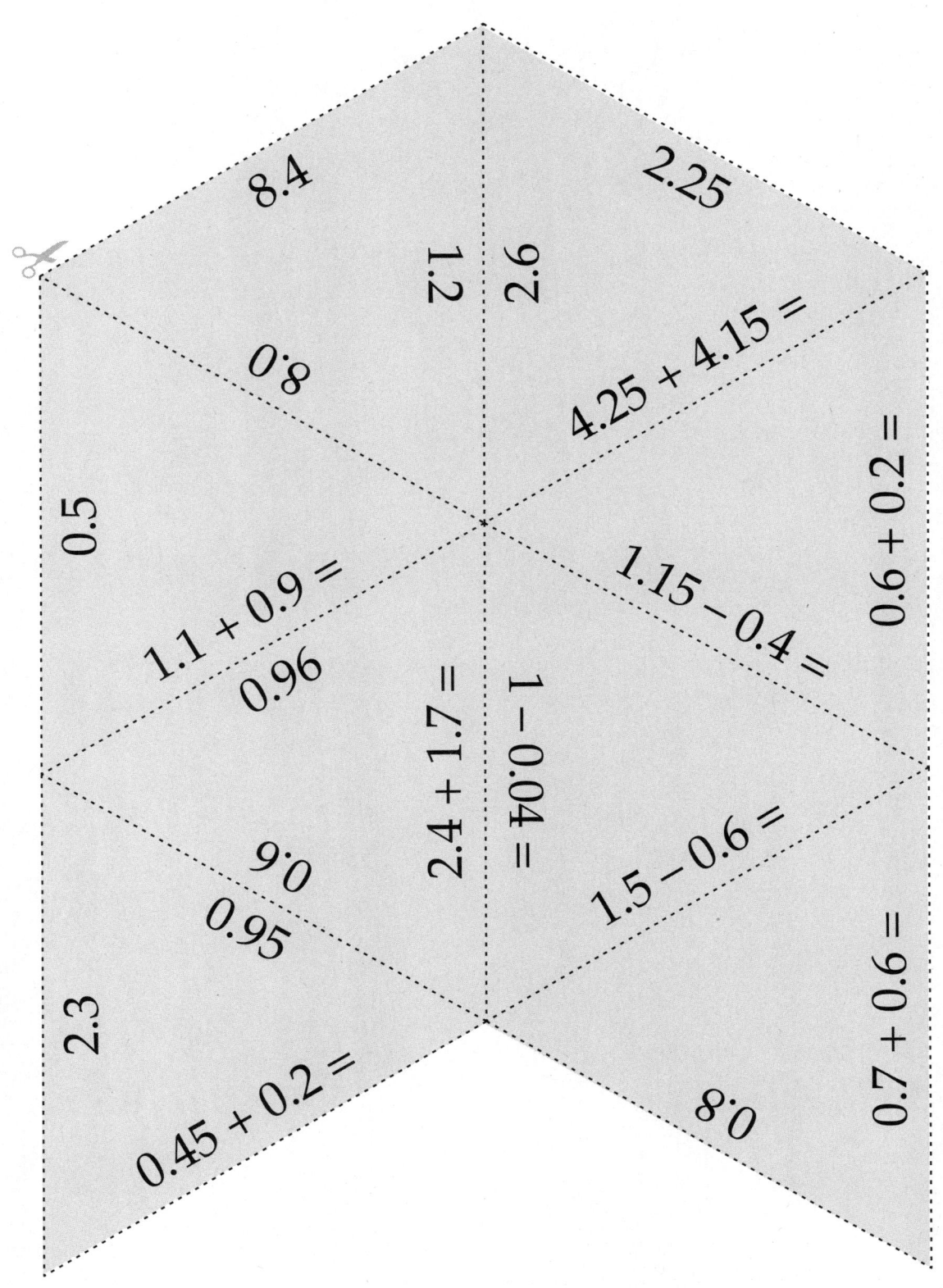

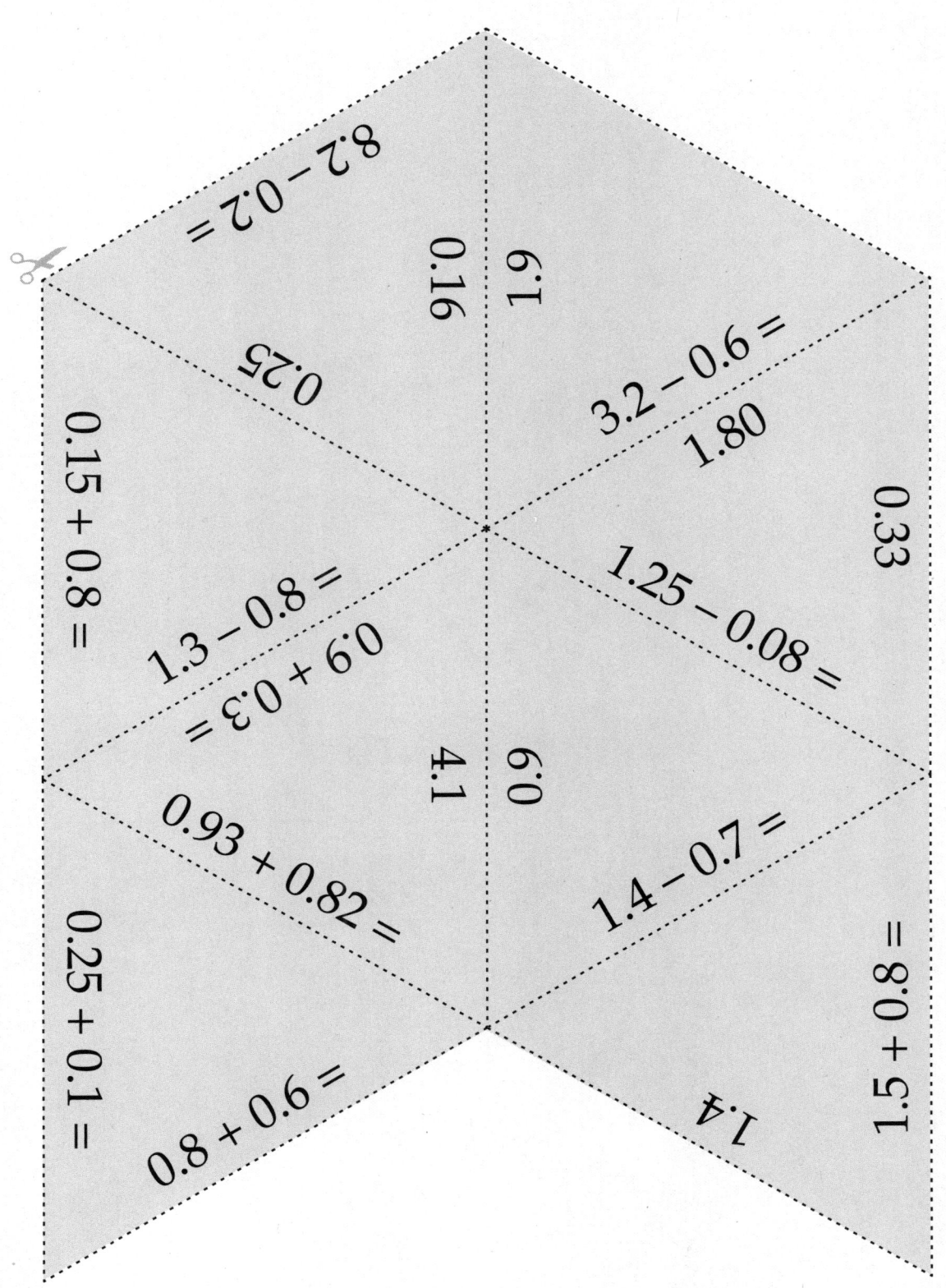

NUMBER LINES

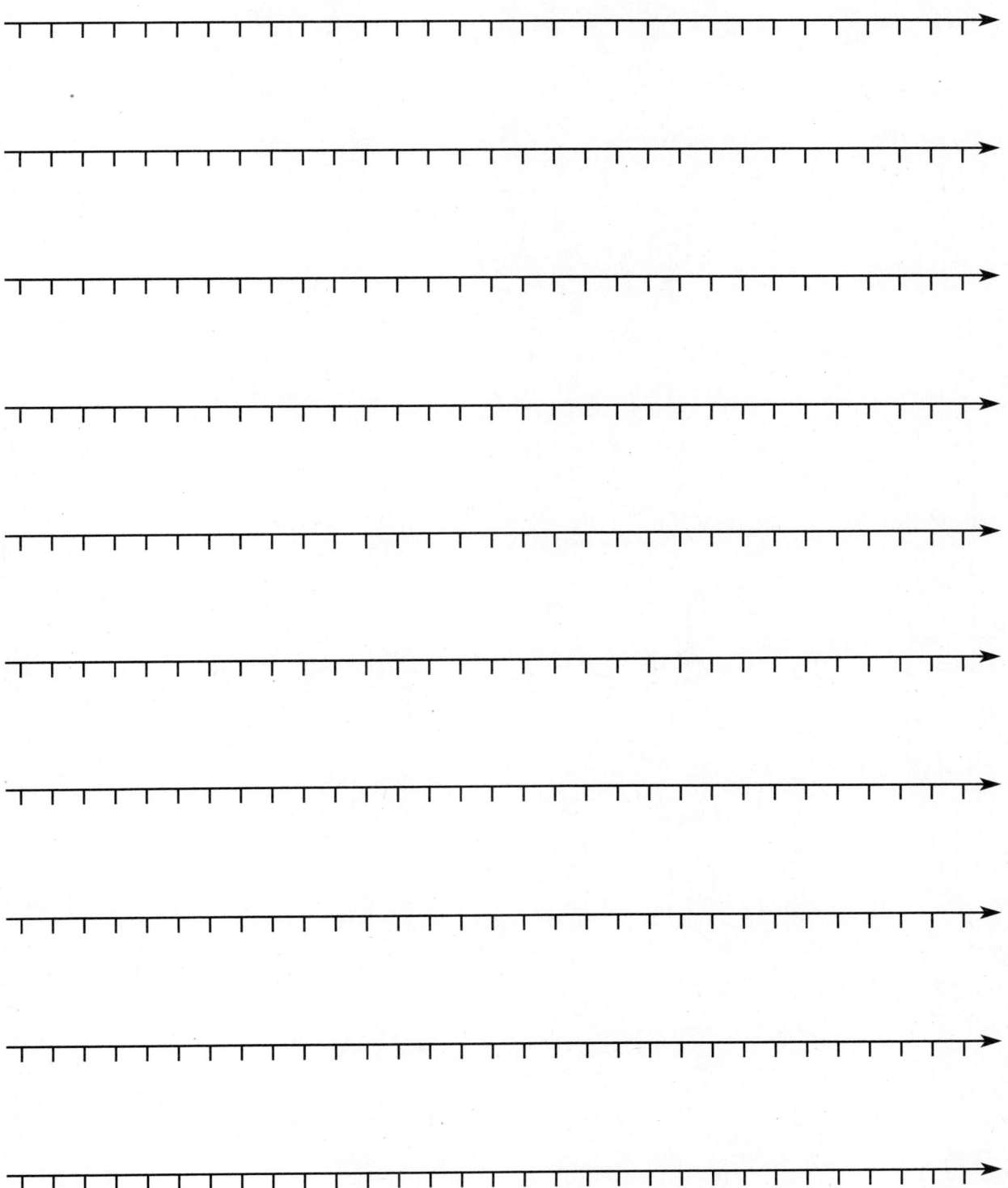

show me

Show me an equation in which you subtract two decimal numbers. One of the numbers should have one decimal place (tenths) and the other should have two decimal places (hundredths).

reflection

The thing I found most helpful for putting together the hexagon puzzle was…

Multiplying Decimals

⤷ **show me**

Use this place-value table to answer questions that your teacher will ask. Write your answers on your response boards.

0.001	0.002	0.003	0.004	0.005	0.006	0.007	0.008	0.009
0.01	0.02	0.03	0.04	0.05	0.06	0.07	0.08	0.09
0.1	0.2	0.3	0.4	0.5	0.6	0.7	0.8	0.9
1	2	3	4	5	6	7	8	9
10	20	30	40	50	60	70	80	90
100	200	300	400	500	600	700	800	900
1,000	2,000	3,000	4,000	5,000	6,000	7,000	8,000	9,000

Show me what you can do to the number 0.9 to get 9,000.

FRACTIONS AND DECIMALS

35 Multiplying Decimals

▷ work time

1. Work with a partner.
   You will need scissors, tape, and a calculator.

   - Get the *How Many Times Bigger?* page (page 207).

   - Cut out all the cards.

   - Get the *Objects, Measurements,* and *Exponential Numbers* cards (pages 209, 211, and 213) and cut out all the cards.

   - Take turns matching an object with its corresponding measurement and the measurement written in exponential form. Tape the matching cards together.

   - Take turns placing an arrow card between the sets of matched cards to show how many times greater in size one object is than the next smaller object.

   - When you place an arrow, explain to your partner how you know that the arrow card goes there.

   - Your partner should either agree with your explanation or challenge it if it is not clear, correct, and complete.

   - When you agree, tape the cards and arrows together.

   - Check your answers with a calculator.

2. What have you learned about multiplying and dividing using powers of ten?

HOW MANY TIMES BIGGER?

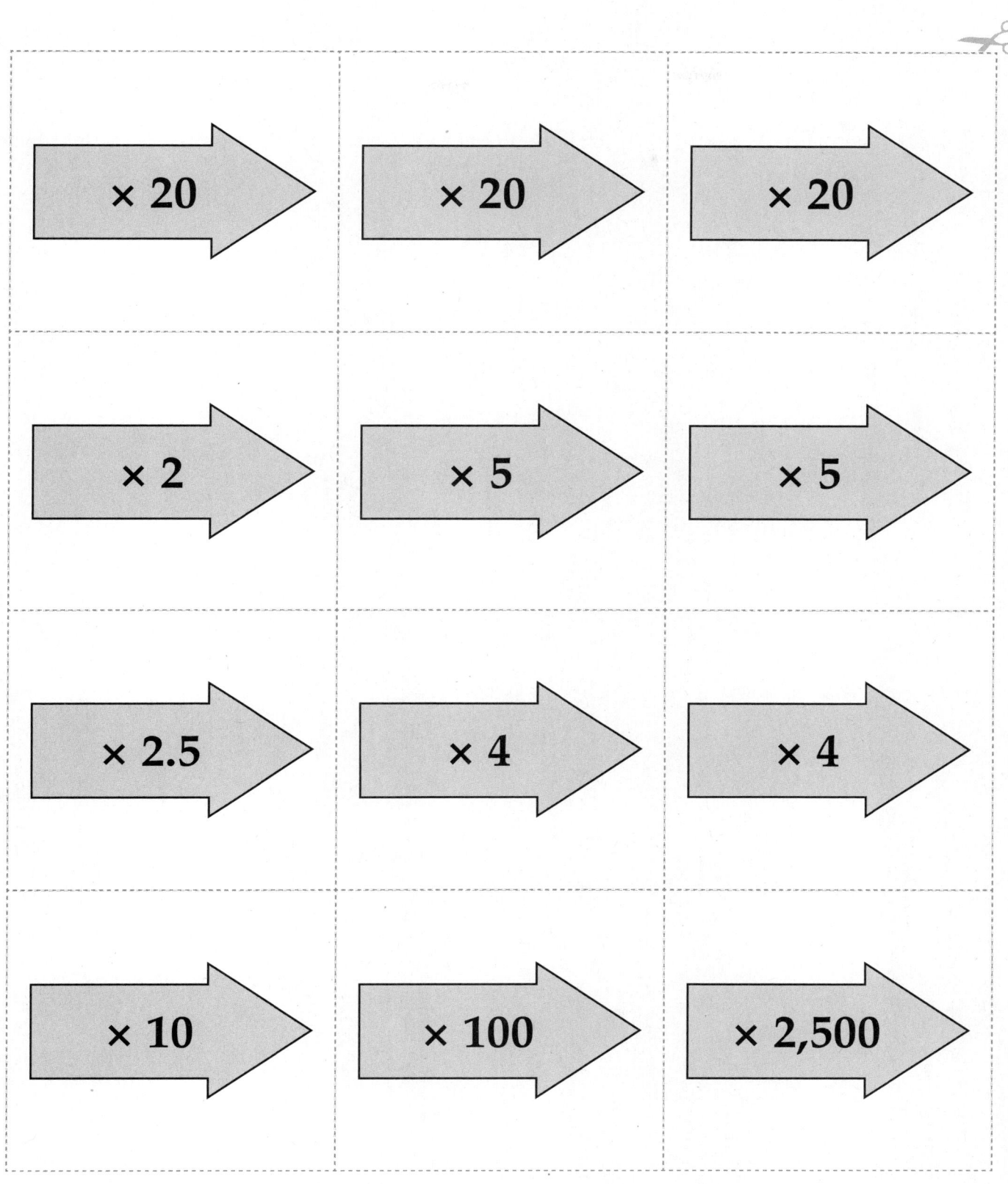

OBJECTS

Wingspan of a jet aircraft 	Length of a stapler 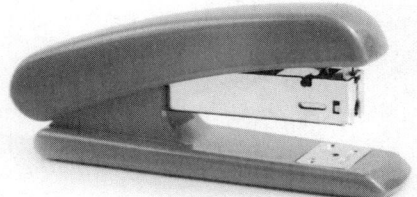	Height of a door 
Length of a truck 	Height of a mountain 	Diameter of the eye of a fly 
Height of a tall skyscraper 	Height of a desk 	Length of a telephone 
Width of a thumb 	Distance from the Earth to the Moon	Distance between two farthest places on Earth 

FRACTIONS AND DECIMALS

MEASUREMENTS

0.2 m	0.02 m	20,000,000 m
400 m	0.8 m	400,000,000 m
8,000 m	0.001 m	40 m
10 m	2 m	0.1 m

EXPONENTIAL NUMBERS

4×10^2 m	1×10^{-3} m	1×10^{-1} m
4×10^8 m	2×10^{-1} m	8×10^3 m
2×10^0 m	1×10^1 m	2×10^{-2} m
4×10^1 m	2×10^7 m	8×10^{-1} m

3. Why is the place-value table on page 205 useful for working with powers of ten?

4. Is 100 a multiple of 10, a power of ten, or both? Explain your answer.

reflection

I think multiples of 10 are like powers of ten because…

I think multiples of 10 are different from powers of ten because…

Multiplying and Dividing Decimals

setting the direction

Review and identify the various strategies described for multiplying and dividing decimal numbers on pages 222–225.

You will use each of these strategies to solve at least one problem in this lesson.

work time

Work with a partner. You are not allowed to use a calculator.

- Work each problem individually. Show your calculations.
- In solving the problems, use each strategy described on pages 222–225 at least once.
- Compare your work with your partner. If you used different strategies, take turns explaining why you chose the strategy you chose.
- Confirm that you got the same results or correct your work as needed.

1. a. 35.7 × 1.82

   b. 35.7 × 18.2

c. 0.357×182

d. 3.57×108.2

e. 357×0.0182

2. a. $288 \div 12$ b. $288 \div 1.2$

c. 288 ÷ 0.12

d. 28.8 ÷ 12

e. 28.8 ÷ 0.12

f. 0.288 ÷ 1.2

g. 0.288 ÷ 0.12

36 Multiplying and Dividing Decimals

3. When is multiplying by $\frac{10}{10}$ or $\frac{100}{100}$ a good strategy for calculations with decimals? Explain how it makes the calculation easier. Explain why this strategy does not change the value of the answer.

4. Show how you can use the distributive property to do at least one of the calculations in today's lesson.

show me

Fill in the blanks with the correct the denominators.

$$3.5 \times 0.12 = \frac{35}{\boxed{}} \times \frac{12}{\boxed{}} = \frac{420}{\boxed{}}$$

reflection

The strategy for dividing decimals I like best is …

because …

36 Multiplying and Dividing Decimals

Multiplying a Decimal by a Whole Number

When you multiply a decimal by a whole number, the number of places to the right of the decimal point will be the same in the answer as in the original decimal number. Just multiply the digits in the usual way, and then place the decimal point in the correct place.

> **example**
>
> $0.25 \times 3 = \dfrac{25}{100} \times 3 = \dfrac{25 \times 3}{100} = \dfrac{75}{100} = 0.75$
>
> Shown in a column, this would be:
>
> $\quad\quad$ 0.25 $\quad$ (two decimal places in this number)
> $\quad\times\ \ \ 3$
> $\quad\quad$ 0.75 $\quad$ (two decimal places in the answer)

If the decimal number has 0s to the right of the decimal point, you may need to add 0s to your answer as placeholders so that the answer will have the same number of places to the right of the decimal point.

> **example**
>
> $0.002 \times 8 = \dfrac{2}{1000} \times 8 = \dfrac{2 \times 8}{1000} = \dfrac{16}{1000} = 0.016$
>
> Shown in a column, this would be:
>
> $\quad\quad$ 0.002 $\quad$ (three decimal places in this number)
> $\quad\times\ \ \ \ 8$
> $\quad\quad$ 0.016 $\quad$ (three decimal places in the answer)

Multiplying Two Decimal Numbers

When you multiply two decimal numbers together, the number of places to the right of the decimal point in the answer will be equal to the sum of the number of places for the two numbers you are multiplying. It may be necessary to add 0s to your answer as placeholders.

> **example**
>
> $$0.002 \times 0.03 = \frac{2}{1000} \times \frac{3}{100} = \frac{6}{100{,}000} = 0.00006$$

> **example**
>
> $3.52 \times 0.04 =$
>
> 3.52 (two places to the right of the decimal point)
> $\underline{\times\ 0.04}$ (two places to the right of the decimal point)
> 0.1408 (four places to the right of the decimal point—the sum of the places above)

36 Multiplying and Dividing Decimals

Dividing a Decimal by a Whole Number

When dividing a decimal number by a whole number, first ignore the decimal point in the dividend and divide as you would two whole numbers. Then put the decimal point in the quotient directly over the decimal point in the dividend. (Remember, in the division problem 10 ÷ 2 = 5, 10 is the dividend, 2 is the divisor, and 5 is the quotient.)

> **example**
>
> 21.76 ÷ 32 =
>
> First divide:
> ```
>        68
> 32)2176
>    192
>    ---
>     256
>     256
>     ---
>       0
> ```
>
> Then put in the decimal points:
> ```
>        0.68
> 32)21.76
>    19 2
>    ----
>     2 56
>     2 56
>     ----
>        0
> ```

If you run out of numbers in the dividend and you have a remainder (as in the example below, there is a reminder of 1), add a 0 to the right of the dividend and continue dividing.

> **example**
>
> 3.85 ÷ 2 =
>
> ```
>      1925
> 2)3.850
>   2
>   --
>   18
>   18
>   --
>    5
>    4
>    --
>    10
>    10
>    --
>     0
> ```
> You still put the decimal point in the dividend so that the value remains the same, (that is, 3.850 = 3.85).
>
> ```
>      1.925
> 2)3.850
>   2
>   --
>   18
>   18
>   --
>    5
>    4
>    --
>    10
>    10
>    --
>     0
> ```
> The decimal point is placed in the quotient just above the decimal point in the dividend.

FRACTIONS AND DECIMALS

Dividing One Decimal by Another Decimal

Suppose you want to calculate 4.76 ÷ 2.8.

Write the division as a fraction, then multiply both numerator and denominator by a power of 10 to change the denominator into a whole number.

example

$$4.76 \div 2.8 = \frac{4.76}{2.8} \times \frac{10}{10}$$ Multiplying by $\frac{10}{10} = 1$ does not change the value.

$$= \frac{47.6}{28}$$

Now divide the decimal by the whole number.

$$4.76 \div 2.8 = \frac{4.76}{2.8}$$

```
      1.7
28)47.6
   28
   ‾‾‾
   19 6
   19 6
   ‾‾‾
      0
```

example

$$8.925 \div 2.55 = \frac{8.925}{2.55} \times \frac{100}{100} = \frac{892.5}{255}$$

```
        3.5
255)892.5
    765
    ‾‾‾‾
    127 5
    127 5
    ‾‾‾‾
        0
```

To summarize:

To divide a decimal number by another decimal number, multiply by $\frac{10}{10}, \frac{100}{100}, \frac{1000}{1000},$ or any fraction equal to 1 so that the denominator becomes a whole number.
Then proceed as you would with dividing by a whole number.

Decimal Operations Word Problems

work time

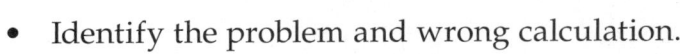

1. Angela has written calculations to show how she would solve each of the six problems below. Your task is to check her work because she has made errors in three of the problems.

   For each incorrect calculation, use the table on page 228 to:
   - Identify the problem and wrong calculation.
   - Think about why Angela might have made the mistake.
   - Provide the correct calculation and correct answer with units.
   - Create a new problem to give Angela more practice working with similar numbers in a similar situation.
   - Provide a correct answer to the problem you created.

a. A car travels 120 miles in 3.6 hours. What is its average speed in miles per hour?		120 ÷ 3.6
b. A snail travels 0.8 miles in 40 hours. What is its average speed in miles per hour?		40 ÷ 0.8
c. Mrs. Abir buys some apples at $1.50 per pound. She spends $3.50. How many pounds does she buy?		3.50 ÷ 1.50
d. Mario buys some tomatoes at $0.90 per pound. He spends 30 cents. How many pounds does he buy?		90 ÷ 30
e. Lena's motorcycle gets 62.5 miles per gallon. How far can she go on 3.4 gallons?		62.5 × 3.4
f. Mr. Okawa's car gets 20 miles per gallon. He only has 0.4 gallons left in the tank. How far will he travel before he runs out of gas?		20 ÷ 0.4

37 Decimal Operations Word Problems

Angela's wrong calculation:	Correct calculation with units:	Correct answer with units:
New problem for Angela:	Correct calculation with units:	Correct answer with units:
Angela's wrong calculation:	Correct calculation with units:	Correct answer with units:
New problem for Angela:	Correct calculation with units:	Correct answer with units:
Angela's wrong calculation:	Correct calculation with units:	Correct answer with units:
New problem for Angela:	Correct calculation with units:	Correct answer with units:

Decimal Operations Word Problems

2. Jin is trying to explain how to solve problem 1f.

"If you cannot decide whether a problem uses multiplying or dividing, then try changing the numbers to easier ones. Just change the 20 to 6 and the 0.4 to 3. Then it is easy to see that the operation should be to multiply."

Misha replies:

"I do not think your method works. If you change the numbers, you might change the operation."

Who is right? Why? Write a reply to these students.

show me

Show me what calculation you need to use in order to find your average speed if you travel 100 miles in 2.5 hours.

reflection

One common mistake people make when solving word problems is…